Praise for *What's in the Way Is the Way*

"Awakening is powerful medicine. A book to live with, learn from, and treasure." CHRISTIANE NORTHRUP, MD, OB/GYN
physician and author of *Women's Bodies, Women's Wisdom*

"These teachings open you to mystery; they bring freedom, joy, and ease." JACK KORNFIELD
founder of Spirit Rock Meditation Center
and author of *A Path with Heart*

"Buddha said you could look the whole world over and never find anyone more deserving of love than yourself. Mary O'Malley awakens us again and again to the startling wonder of what lies beyond our workable hindrances, the liberation of our luminous nature." STEPHEN LEVINE
author of *A Year to Live*

"This is the most no-nonsense, grounded, accessible spirituality you will ever come across. I love Mary's teachings. They are simple and practical yet awesomely profound, and offer hope to those in even the darkest places. Her message is medicine for the world." JEFF FOSTER
author of *The Deepest Acceptance*

"This beautiful book is filled with heart wisdom. Mary O'Malley's teachings are simple, deep, and profoundly transforming . . . they will guide you in letting go and trusting life." TARA BRACH, PHD
author of *Radical Acceptance*

"Mary O'Malley's book shares meaningful information and wisdom. I know from my experience that she speaks the truth, and her guidance can make a significant difference in how we manage our journey through life." BERNIE SIEGEL, MD
author of *Love, Medicine and Miracles*

"Down-to-earth and joyful! Mary's words offer a healing path for all who wish to travel away from self-limiting views toward freedom of heart." SHARON SALZBERG
cofounder of the Insight Meditation Society
and author of *Real Happiness*

"Humans today are being asked to make a profound leap in consciousness. We are the first generation in 200,000 years to know that the universe is not just a space filled with various objects, but is in fact an ongoing creative process. No longer can we think of ourselves as separate individuals trapped in a tiny world. We are in fact a wave of creative energy that has been traveling for 14 billion years. With her new book, *What's in the Way Is the Way*, Mary O'Malley has created a process where each of us can enter into this deep truth of ourselves. By following her lead—by learning to dwell in our deep nature as a daily practice—we come to feel that joy of astonishment that accompanies every great awakening of love."
BRIAN THOMAS SWIMME
California Institute of Integral Studies

"A gentle, loving guide to a happier and more peaceful life. Everyone can benefit from the wise words in this book."
JOSEPH GOLDSTEIN
author of *Mindfulness*

"It is a sincere relief to read a book that so clearly demystifies the precise things which I have been working on lately. With *What's in the Way Is the Way*, Mary O'Malley has scripted a pathway through confusion into the light of our own consciousness. It is chock full of signposts and refuses to allow you to remain lost. This is a book that everyone should read, particularly those whose lives have been touched by addiction (and that is everyone)." TOMMY ROSEN
author of *Recovery 2.0*

"I consider Mary O'Malley to be one of the most extraordinary teachers of our time. No one is more adept at showing us how to turn life's most difficult moments into life's greatest gifts. Her deep compassion, uncommon awareness, and crystal-clear insight make anything she writes a treasure." NEALE DONALD WALSCH
author of *Conversations with God*

"In a world where we are pathologically encouraged to dismiss aspects of our authentic experience, this book is deeply welcome. With beautiful *hearticulation*, Mary O'Malley invites us to give voice to that which has been buried, illuminating pathways for transformation that are desperately needed in this mad world. An invitation to presence. An invitation to inclusivity. The wholly holy. This book comforts me."
JEFF BROWN
author of *Soulshaping*

"I loved Mary's message—for me, born with an overdose of curiosity, it gives new meaning and usefulness to the word!"
ELISABET SAHTOURIS, PHD
evolutionary biologist and futurist

"Mary O'Malley is a genuine master, a sensible, plain-speaking exemplar of spiritual awakening and illuminated guidance. Every word in this book rings true. I loved it." MARK MATOUSEK
author of *When You're Falling, Dive*

"Mary O'Malley has developed a wonderful process to let go of struggle and become more fully alive. She teaches us to use compassionate curiosity to bring insight to the healing of whatever is getting in our way." MARCI SHIMOFF
author of *Happy for No Reason*

"I love the title of Mary's book, *What's in the Way Is the Way*; it says it all. Her wisdom about gentleness and compassion, especially with ourselves, is so essential to take in. We all have a contribution to make to the evolution of peace and healing for our world and—as so many great teachers have said—it needs to start with ourselves. Mary O'Malley offers a timeless teaching. Now, may we each live it to the best of our ability." RICHARD MOSS
author of *The Mandala of Being*

"Mary O'Malley's amazing book is testimony that our most trying challenges bear with them the seeds of our most inspiring triumphs!" AL COLE
CBS radio host of the nationally syndicated talk show *People of Distinction*

"I am just in awe of Mary's work. Mary transforms our everyday challenges into something sacred. Her insights into what it means to be truly human touched my heart so deeply. I think Mary O'Malley is the freshest voice of truth out there today." ANN LOUISE GITTLEMAN, PHD
author of *The Fat Flush Plan*

"Mary offers a graceful and skillful communication, a quality of responsiveness that is seasoned and not commonly seen." JERRY KATZ
founder of nonduality.com and host of Nonduality Talk Radio

"Out of the plentiful garden of books out there on spirituality that get too heady or are not experiential enough to really help people, this rare gem is different. I love how Mary adds just the right combination of explanation and instruction."   SCOTT KILOBY
author and founder of The Kiloby Center for Recovery

"In reading the book and doing the work, I felt as though a thousand pieces became a workable and digestible whole. It is brilliant in its simplicity and unparalleled in its ability to touch that soft spot we all have, the one that says me and my life matter, and we are in this together and not alone."   LORRAINE HURLEY, MD
host of *Uncommon Awareness*
on Dreamvisions 7 Radio Network

"Mary's work is fantastic and so important in helping people on the path to both personal freedom and more wisdom on the planet. Mary's new book brings a vital focus to the intelligence of the heart, to the power of breath, and to the awakening of the human spirit."
GRANT SOOSALU
author of *Avoiding the Enemies to Happiness*

"The title of Mary O'Malley's book, *What's in the Way Is the Way*, says it all. It's a mantra we can repeat. By opening her book to any page, we are reminded of our 'clouds of struggle' and how we can gracefully move out of the struggle and the confines of our limited perceptions. It's a book to take wherever you go."   ANDREA ADLER
author of *The Science of Spiritual Marketing*

"Mary once again offers a gentle clarity that invites us to embrace ourselves and our circumstances, our experiences and our dreams. She invites us to undertake this journey not with willfulness, but willingness. Mary is truly a treasure, the pearl of great and rare value."
JEFF RENNER
chief meteorologist, KING 5 News in Seattle

"This book is a powerful resource for anyone seeking peace, well-being, and freedom from internal struggle." JON GABRIEL
author and founder of The Gabriel Method,
A Mind-Body Approach to Weight Loss

"Reading a book is one thing. Being joyously changed while reading it, right there, on the spot . . . is another. Mary O'Malley does that, repeatedly, and with élan and deep wisdom. She glides you into a consciousness that is alert, realistic, and transformative. Her teaching is direct and full of felt life, quietly guiding you away from disturbing emotions and drifting thoughts of oppression. Her gift to the reader is immeasurable because it is so present and full of the eternal presence."
DAVID SILVER
TV director/writer and cofounder of Mindpod Network

"I love Mary's style. It's obvious that her words come from an honest heart—one that has known both rapture and heartbreak. Mary has learned to live in a way that's open to life. This book shares in a very clear and concise way how you too can learn to use what's in the way as the way to your own personal freedom." CHRIS GROSSO
author of *Everything Mind*

"Mary's book is a laser-like guide for people of all stages in life treading the path of self-inquiry. In plain-spoken words, Mary gives the reader a challenge to change our perspective from ego-based to soul from which we can transform fear into love." RAGHU MARKUS
executive director of Love Serve Remember Foundation
and cofounder of Mindpod Network

What's in the Way
Is the Way

ALSO BY MARY O'MALLEY

The Magical Forest of Aliveness: A Tale of Awakening

Belonging to Life: The Journey of Awakening

The Gift of Our Compulsions:
A Revolutionary Approach to Self-Acceptance and Healing

What's in the Way Is the Way

A PRACTICAL GUIDE *for* WAKING UP TO LIFE

Mary O'Malley

SOUNDS TRUE
BOULDER, COLORADO

Sounds True
Boulder, CO 80306

Published 2016

Cover design by Rachael Murray
Book design by Beth Skelley

Hafiz, "The Sun Never Says," translated by Daniel Ladinsky, from *The Gift: Poems by
Hafiz the Great Sufi Master* (New York: Penguin, 1999). Copyright © 1999 by Daniel
Ladinsky. "My Brilliant Image," translated by Daniel Ladinsky, from *I Heard God
Laughing: Poems of Hope and Joy* (New York: Penguin, 2006). Copyright © 1996, 2006
by Daniel Ladinsky. All reprinted with the permission of The Permissions Company,
Inc., for the translator.

Rumi, "The Guest House," from *The Essential Rumi*, translated by Coleman Barks with
John Moyne (New York: HarperCollins, 1995), 109. Permission to reprint granted by
the translator.

Printed in the United States of America

Library of Congress Cataloging-in-Publication Data
O'Malley, Mary, 1945– author.
   What's in the way is the way : a practical guide for waking up to life / Mary O'Malley.
      pages cm
   ISBN 978-1-62203-524-3
   1. Self-actualization (Psychology) 2. Self-realization. 3. Conduct of life. I. Title.
   BF637.S4O533 2016
   158.1—dc23
                                                    2015030670

Ebook ISBN 978-1-62203-555-7
10 9 8 7 6 5 4 3 2 1

This book is dedicated to MarySue Brooks,
my treasured friend and business partner.
Thank you for living this work and bringing your wisdom to it.
Your presence, your skills, your commitment,
and your heart have been necessary in its unfolding.
Words cannot describe how grateful I am
that we get to walk this path together.

Contents

Foreword

by Neale Donald Walsch

author of *Conversations with God*

When I was a boy, I used to go around saying, "Life is so simple. Why does everyone keep making it so complicated?"

I couldn't understand why all the kids in school would get so kerfuffled when a big test was coming up or when the end-of-year grades were due. I couldn't figure out (even when I was seven, eight, and nine) why Mom and Dad "got into it" so often at home or why Mom worried so much about stuff.

I was never clear about why anyone would be so concerned or worried about anything that they'd let themselves shift from cheerfulness to snippiness, from happiness to grouchiness, from inner peace to inward anxiety.

For some reason, I always knew things would work out—and they always did. Maybe they didn't always work out the way I thought they would or exactly the way I wanted them to, but they always worked out in a way that brought me to my next highest good—and it didn't take me long to catch on to what was happening and to begin to depend on this being simply "The Way Life Is."

Now, wonderful spiritual teacher Mary O'Malley has written a whole book about this—explaining it clearly and in wonderfully accessible terms.

I'm so excited about this book! I consider it to be one of the most important pieces of writing to come our way in a very long time, and it absolutely will be—of this I am sure—one of the most beneficial books you have ever read.

This book talks about how to deal with life exactly as it is occurring, not just when it's easy to do so, but when it's the most difficult—which, irony of ironies, makes it easy to do so.

And as much as I thought I knew about all this, boy could I have used this book when I was moving through the worst days of my personal journey. As with all of us, there have been some pretty tough ones. And in those moments we can easily forget—or at least I did—whatever we thought we knew about how to navigate the rocky shoals of life.

If in those moments I could have had something that I could turn to, something that could have helped me understand what was going on and how to get through it, I would have given anything. And if I had had something that I could refer to ahead of time so that I might have a specific approach to dealing with challenging moments, I would have considered it the biggest blessing of my life.

I can promise you that you will never find life more clearly explained than it is here, nor will you have placed in your hands more useful or powerful tools with which to negotiate its most difficult experiences.

It is true for me that as a child I seemed to know, intuitively, that life need not be as utterly discombobulating as I was observing people experiencing it, but I could not have told you why that was so—much less how to make it so. Mary O'Malley has done both here and thus produced one of the greatest gifts one human being could offer to another.

If this is a challenging time in your life (or if someone you know and love is moving through a challenging moment in theirs), you could not have been led to a more perfect resource than this book—nor to a more compassionate, understanding, spiritually aware, emotionally articulate, psychologically brilliant, and wonderfully able and capable messenger and teacher than its author.

Put simply, this book will show you the way to a better life, without needing a single thing to be different for you to retain your inner peace, your outer joy, and your overall well-being. Yet it is far from a theory book or a concept document. It is a practitioner's guide. It is an easy-to-follow instruction book. It could easily have been titled *Life's Operating Manual*.

Your soul knew exactly what it was doing when it brought you here. (You know, of course, that you did not "stumble upon" this book by chance.) Absorb it, then. Inhale it. Drink it in as the nectar of the gods. For it is surely from Divinity Itself that flows such wisdom as is here.

Thank you, Mary O'Malley, for our days and nights are enriched by you and our wounded places are healed.

Introduction

Your Transformation Begins

I am inviting you on the most important journey you will ever take: the journey back to a heartfelt connection with yourself and a trust-filled connection with your life. This journey will show you that there is a sense of well-being with you always, no matter what is happening in your life.

If you are like most people, you have only sporadic glimpses of this well-being. This may be because you, like most everyone else, have a deep belief inside of you that says you are not enough. You may also have been conditioned to believe that if you just fix yourself or your life, you will be "enough" and thus know the peace and happiness you long for. You have become an ongoing project, and this causes you to struggle with your compulsions, your finances, your relationships, and your health. Rather than peace and joy, you may very well be living with a low-grade sense of unease that periodically flares up and plunges you into turmoil. Your life has become a series of problems to be solved rather than an adventure to be lived. If you are honest with yourself, you recognize that this fixing game has never brought you peace, well-being, or ease.

I too lived from this place of struggle for many years, so I intimately know the deep pain and heartache that comes from the fix-it mode. I was very compulsive, at times suicidal, and felt that I had no value. Most of the time, I experienced a sense of unease, and often it would flare up into dread, hopeless despair, and overall anxiousness. These feelings would show up as relentless struggles in my mind, knots in my stomach, and debilitating headaches that came from an intense longing to run away from my life. I gained a huge amount of weight, washed a lot of the food down with alcohol, and took every pill I could get my hands on.

Since I perceived myself as defective, I tried to get rid of the parts of me I didn't like and hold on to the ones I did. But these parts seemed to have a life of their own, appearing when I didn't want them and disappearing when I wanted them to stay. I also desperately tried to understand it all, but that just kept me caught in my head.

It wasn't until I discovered how to listen to myself that I began to open up again. Rather than always being in fix-it mode, I learned how to meet myself exactly as I am, opening into the place beyond judging, fixing, getting rid of, and trying to understand. I learned the art of being present for my own experience, no matter what it is, and the art of meeting myself—even the so-called unacceptable, unmeetable parts of myself—in my own heart.

Slowly, just as the morning light dispels the dark, I came back to myself. I also discovered how to show up for the great adventure of Life—not just life in the everyday sense, but the intelligent process unfolding in and through everyone and everything. Instead of always trying to create a better reality, I showed up for Reality with a capital R. (When capitalized, the words *Life* and *Reality*—as well as *Love, Intelligence,* and *Presence*—all refer to the interconnected, intelligent field of being that is Life.)

Rather than being in a constant state of unease, I came to know more and more joy, trust, and love. Did this make all of my vulnerabilities go away? No. These feelings will always be a part of me, for vulnerability is an essential part of being human, and vulnerabilities are the doorways back into peace, joy, and love. Now mine are nestled in the spaciousness of my own heart. And when they get reawakened through this sometimes fierce process called Life, they don't take over any more. Instead, they open my heart even more.

I tell you this so that you know what I am offering you here comes from having actually lived it. Rather than letting me stay lost in the depth of darkness I'd taken on, Life itself showed me the pathway from contraction and struggle to connection and well-being. Since I began sharing my journey more than thirty years ago, I have guided thousands of people on their own journeys back to themselves and back to Life. And each of them, in turn, has helped me to see more clearly the pathway back to Life.

In this book, I am inviting you on a journey back to ease and well-being. In this exploration, you will first discover how to see through the game of struggle so you can know the joy of being fully alive. Struggle is like a cloud bank of stories that cuts you off from your natural state of joy and peace, and you have been conditioned throughout your life to believe in these stories. Struggle is based on fear; it is held together with judgment, and it leaves you vulnerable to sadness, anger, loneliness, and despair. Your struggling self doesn't only grapple with the big challenges of Life; it resists the smaller things, like the length of the stoplight, the spot on your shirt, or the shape of your nose. You will learn how not to get seduced by your mind's addiction to struggle, how to see the particular stories of struggle you were conditioned to believe, and how to give them the spacious acceptance they need to let go. You will learn how to unhook from all of the fears, longings, irritations, and sorrows that struggle generates. Rather than turning to your compulsions or fighting with the people in your life, you will be able to simply let it all pass through you, knowing that at any given moment only a small part of you has a problem with Life. The rest of you is at peace.

You will also learn how to meet yourself exactly as you are, weaving every part of yourself—even the parts you think are unlikable and unlovable—into your own heart. You will move beyond being a victim of the challenges of your life so that you can gather the treasures that always accompany them. You will come to see that your life, rather than being a series of events that are happening *to* you, is all happening *for* you. Everything in your life—especially your challenges—is tailor-made to help you see your stories of struggle. Whatever is in the way *is* the way! You will learn how to listen to your challenges, rather than striving to overcome them, so they can lead you back to your heart.

And finally, you will rediscover how to be open to Life again—right here, right now, feeling at home no matter where you are, no matter what is happening. Everything you experience on this journey will allow you the safety to show up for the great adventure called Life—not an idea of what it should be, but the real thing. This is what you deeply long for: an intimate connection with Life. At your core, you yearn to show up for what Life is offering in this moment rather than wanting your experience to be different than it is. You long to let go of trying, resisting, and constantly evaluating how you're doing so that you can relax into your life and know the joy of being fully available and present for Life.

Joseph Campbell, the much-loved mythologist and writer, said in *The Power of Myth*, "People say that what we're all seeking is a meaning for life. I don't think that's what we're really seeking. I think what we're seeking is an experience of being alive, so that our life experiences on the purely physical plane will have resonance within our own innermost being and reality, so that we actually feel the rapture of being alive. That's what it's all finally about."

What Campbell is alluding to is the heart of this book. It is an invitation to fully experience Life so you can again know "the rapture of being alive," which is all about connecting with what is right here, right now.

Chapter 1 shows you how your stories of struggle become clouds in your mind that eventually surround you, cutting you off from seeing the meadow of your own innate okayness and from Life. You will also meet "the storyteller," the voice that spins the ongoing tales of struggle, and discover the power of compassionate curiosity to quiet your storyteller. In chapter 2, we explore the qualities of the meadow in more detail. Chapter 3 examines fear, which is the core movement of your storyteller, and you'll discover that it is possible to see through its stories. In chapter 4, you take the essential step of discovering that you are not the one in charge of this transformation process, you are not alone, and help is only a question away.

With this foundation, in chapter 5 we'll explore the power of being curious about your immediate experience. Chapter 6 guides you in discovering *how* to bring the power of curiosity into your daily life.

In chapter 7 we look at your heart's ability to heal. Then, in chapter 8, you'll learn how to touch even the deepest of holdings inside of you with the healing of your heart.

In chapter 9 you will reconnect with your natural state of trust. In chapter 10, all that we have explored will be brought together into four guidelines that will help you to be with whatever Life brings you. By the end of this book, you will discover that what we are exploring in these pages has the power to transform the world.

HOW TO GET THE MOST FROM THIS BOOK

Understanding what is being offered here is an important step, but the doors into being fully alive open through *experiencing* what is being offered. You may have some resistance to opening to Life, for while this is what we all deeply long for, we are also afraid of it. Direct experience, even of the resistant part of you, can help you get past any resistance that may come up. In this book, I have incorporated two means of helping you move through resistance and connect with the truth beyond the words.

First, throughout each chapter, you will be invited to pause to connect with what is being offered in that moment. These are invitations to let go of the world of struggle and open to Life here and now, to dip the finger of your attention into the river of your experience and let Life in. You can stay at just the level of understanding the words, and that can be an important phase. But there comes a time when we become ready to move beyond understanding into actually experiencing what the words are pointing to. You don't have to figure out what that is; you simply discover that you can let go of the game of struggle and connect with Life in the moment.

Second, I have designed a ten-week introspective process to allow you to fully experience the offerings of each of the ten chapters. This process is found in the section called "Remembering" at the end of each chapter. This name reflects that everything offered in this book you already know and have just forgotten. But this process also contains an element of re-membering: we no longer see ourselves as a separated part of a dismembered whole, but rediscover the cohesiveness of Life and how we are necessary components of it. The more we clear out our stories of struggle, the more we re-member, or put ourselves back into, this great flow of Life.

You will be given a "Remembering Statement" that captures the essence of what was explored in each chapter. These truth statements come from the place beyond the struggling self. They will help you, as you move throughout your day, to reconnect with what you have learned. You can write the truths on sticky notes and place them around your environment. Or you can associate them with something you do many times a day, such as using the bathroom or answering the phone. You can even use them as a mantra during your times of conscious breathing.

These truths will also be helpful in getting to know your struggling self, which may at times argue with the core remembering. Notice when your mind is open to them, and notice what it says when it is not. Remember that when your mind is arguing with a truthful statement, this is just your struggling self.

If the statement that is chosen for the week doesn't call to you, ask yourself what touched you the most in the chapter. Then put it in a few words that you can come back to throughout the week, reminding yourself what you are remembering.

You are also encouraged to spend some quiet time with yourself every day, learning to see and listen to your inner experiences rather than being seduced by the game of struggle. I call these times "Remembering Sessions." Through them, you are invited to bring what we are exploring in each chapter into your immediate experience.

These sessions may look like meditation, but in the traditional sense, they are not. Rather than trying to make something happen or get to a better state or change what is, you are strengthening the muscle of your attention. With attention, you can be curious about what is going on right now in order to discover how to relate to your immediate experience rather than turning it into a problem. For it is when your attention and your immediate experience come together that you rediscover your innate sense of ease, peace, and well-being beyond the clouds of struggle in your mind.

Your Remembering Session is a powerful place to get to know your mind. If you are like most people, your mind will have times when it struggles with the sessions. It will try to do them right and judge itself for how it is doing. It will often get bored or just space out. Most people think they are failures at what is called "meditation" because they're trying to do it "right." But your experience would be completely different if you knew that whatever shows up in your daily Remembering Session is exactly what needs to be there, and that when you can be curious about it, you step out of the game of struggle.

On the first day of each week, I suggest you read through the instructions for the chapter's Remembering Session and then close your eyes and go exploring. The abbreviated version at the end of the instructions can guide you for every day of the week after that.

Many people find it helpful to connect with themselves in this way as early in the day as they can, so it sets a tone for the day. If this doesn't work for you, find a time when you can regularly explore the Remembering Session of the chapter.

You can also sprinkle a minute or two of becoming curious about what you are experiencing as you move throughout your day. As with the Remembering Statements, it can help to connect this curiosity with something you do a number of times during the day, like eating, using the bathroom, or answering the phone.

I have designed the Remembering process to span ten weeks, so you can spend seven days connecting with the core discoveries of each chapter and your experience of them. But I encourage you to take more or less time, as you feel called to. You could spend several weeks on one session or move through two in one week. Also, while the sessions do help you integrate on a deeper level what is being offered here, if you are not called to do the sessions, honor that. You will still receive from the book what you need to receive. Trust yourself and open to these sessions if and when it is right for you. Even though there is a tried-and-true pathway from *doing* Life to *being* Life, you have your unique expression of that path. So it is important that you take in what resonates with you and leave the rest.

*

The core of our journey together is about opening what has been closed inside of you, so that the energy that has been bound up in your struggling self can be released and you can again know the joy of being fully alive. Well-being is here right now. You don't need to search for it, you don't need to fix yourself to know it, and you don't even need to change anything in your life. Your innate sense of well-being is revealed as you learn how to unhook from your struggling self.

On behalf of all the people who live on this beautiful, blue-green jewel that is our planet, I thank you for your willingness to take this journey back to Life. This gratitude comes from knowing that as you discover and live from the meadow of well-being, your life will be transformed. And as your life transforms, you will transform the lives of everybody you meet—or even think about—for the rest of your life. When you are not caught in the world of struggle, you are *here*, open to the amazing majesty and mystery of Life, radiating the presence of well-being. And a human being who has discovered how to be here becomes an invitation to all beings to unhook from the mind's addiction to struggle and open back into the joy of being fully here for Life. For the healing of all beings, Life is bringing you home.

Are you ready to embark on the journey from struggle to well-being? If so, let's begin.

1

It's All Okay—It's Truly Okay

I magine a day when everything was okay—not just okay, but *really* okay. You may have just fallen in love or received something you have wanted for a long time. Or maybe you are on vacation with no pressures, lying on a beach in deep contentment. Allow the images of your okay day to fill you up. Go for the gusto—let in that *okayness.* Let it flood your mind, your body, and your heart.

Now notice what you are experiencing as you use your imagination to open up to the joy of everything being okay. In your mind there is probably a sense that nothing needs to be any different than it is. In your body, there is likely an experience of deep relaxation that allows for the glow of joy. Your heart is open, spacious, and light. *Ahh!*

What would it be like if you knew that everything was always okay? That doesn't mean there wouldn't be challenges. It just means that you wouldn't turn them into problems, so then you would be able to respond to them from a clear place. What would it be like to live from this open, relaxed, engaged, and spacious place? Isn't this what you deeply long for—to no longer struggle with Life and instead be available to the experience of Life as it is right here, right now? This is possible! In fact, everything in your life is a part of the journey into recognizing and living from a place that is beyond struggle.

THE MYTH OF NOT BEING OKAY

We all long for this okayness, and yet it seems very elusive. If you step back and look at what is going on inside of you all day long, you would see that rather than resting in the ease of okayness, your mind is often doing the opposite. It is searching for something better—a better body, a better mate, a better meditation, a better car, a better mind. This kind of mind hopes that if you can just get your life the way you want it to be, then you will feel okay.

You can also spend a lot of energy trying to get rid of the parts of you that you don't like. You hope all of this wanting and resisting will finally soothe the raging beast of the voice in your head that says you and your life need to be different than what they are in order to have everything be okay. When struggling with your life doesn't bring you lasting satisfaction, you look for it through the numbing world of compulsions.

When you look honestly at your search for a better experience, you will see that it doesn't work. Or the better way to say it is that it does work, for brief moments, but it keeps you caught in the belief that if you just do it right—if you change yourself and your life enough—then you will know that illusive okayness you so deeply long for. But haven't you noticed that every time your mind feels that it has gotten yourself and your life together, they haven't stayed that way?

It is very important to understand that the mind is not being put down here. It is an exquisite creation of Life that took 13.8 billion years to form—since the beginning of the universe. Life created the mind as a tool for maneuvering through Life, not to be in charge of it. The mind is a wonderful servant, but it is a horrible master. Giving it the task of being in charge of Life has created the world of struggle that most people live in all day long, keeping them cut off from peace and joy.

The more you can learn how to use your mind rather than having it use you, you will discover that okayness is your natural state and that it is always with you no matter what happens in your life. You just don't see it because you are always trying to find it. And you can't find it, for you have never lost it. You could be angry, deeply despairing, or even very afraid, and your natural field of well-being is also there at the same moment you are caught in struggle. You can learn how to recognize and live from the place beyond struggle, no matter what is happening in your life.

❦ Close your eyes for a moment and listen. There are all sorts of sounds happening right now. To keep your mind engaged, count how many different ones you can hear. When you are done, open your eyes and recognize something very amazing: for a moment, your intention wasn't to think about Life. It was to directly experience it by listening to it. There is a big difference between thinking about Life and actually experiencing it. ❧

THE MEADOW

Imagine a beautiful meadow on a sunlit morning. In this meadow is a rainbow of wildflowers, along with the heart-opening music of birds. The smells of the heather and the pristine beauty of the surrounding mountains bring forth a deep sense of peace.

This meadow represents the experience of okayness that is at the heart of Life, and because you are a part of this wonderful, mysterious unfolding that is Life, the meadow is at the core of your being too. You knew and lived in this okayness when you were very young. You may have no memories of this kind of well-being, but there was a time when there were no thoughts in your head. Past and future had no meaning for you, so this moment was all there was. Because you weren't searching for a better state, you were open to Life—all of it—and Life was okay exactly as it was. Even when there was pain and discomfort, you fully experienced it rather than turning it into a problem in your mind.

Now imagine yourself as a young child living in the meadow, fascinated by the newness of every moment, open to everything. Clouds in the sky come and go, as do laughter and tears, so everything inside of you and outside of you flows.

As you grow, thoughts begin to fill your head as you start to tell yourself stories about yourself and about Life.

Clouds in the sky begin to lower and circle around your head. At first they are just wispy clouds that don't fully block your experience of the meadow. But over time, usually by adolescence, the clouds completely surround you and fill your head, so much so that you can no longer see the meadow. All you can see are the ever-shifting clouds in your mind.

This is where most people live: in a cloud of ideas about Life. And most of the time they struggle with Life rather than directly experiencing it. Most of the struggles are small—not liking how your hair looks or the length of the stoplight—but sometimes struggles become so big that they end up in loneliness and despair. When you were young and first saw a bird, you saw it in all of its mystery. You experienced it not as an object of your mind but as a living experience all throughout your being. As you grew up, you began to experience it as a thought: "Oh, that is a bird." As you became more and more caught in thoughts about Life rather than directly experiencing Life, you were slowly conditioned to struggle with Life: liking/disliking, wanting/resisting, should/should not, good/bad, right/wrong. And struggle is what makes up the clouds that separate you from the meadow of okayness at the heart of Life.

It may be difficult for you to see that you are identified with the clouds in your mind because it has been a while since you spent an extended period of time in the meadow of well-being within you. Like most people, you have probably become used to chronic, low-grade struggles—to believing that your thoughts are true and that if you could only get those thoughts to be the way you want them to be, then everything would be okay. You can win the lottery, think happy thoughts until the cows come home, meditate for hours every day to find the states of mind you like, get plastic surgery to make your body look "perfect," yet none of that is enough, because *all of these things are not the meadow.* They are just attempts to find the meadow, and they will only thicken your clouds in the long run, leading to still more struggle.

THE STORYTELLER

The storyteller is the voice of your clouds of struggle. You know what I mean—that voice in your head that talks all day. If you had a little door on your forehead that you could open up, you would see the storyteller voicing an opinion about everything. It comments on what it likes and what it doesn't like. It tells you what you should do and shouldn't do, and often it changes from one to the other in a matter of seconds. It judges unmercifully—not only other people, but also yourself. And it is afraid—afraid of Life, afraid of its own fear, and deeply afraid of being alone.

Because the storyteller is constantly trying to do everything right, it manipulates, tries, expects, wants, rages, and resists. It generates all sorts of feelings, such as fear, sadness, self-judgment, anger, doubt, confusion, irritation, and despair to name just a few. It also generates feelings of love, kindness, and peace, but these usually show up only when the storyteller is getting what it wants. As soon as it doesn't, any feelings that generate from the heart are usually closed down.

If you watch closely, you will see that the storyteller is lost in an endless game of struggle—struggles with everyday things like the length of the line at the grocery store, the color of your new makeup, your mate changing the TV channel, the two pounds you gained. But at times it leads you into big struggles, such as "He rejected me, and I can't stand to be alone," "I found a lump in my breast and am going to die," "If I don't get a job, I will lose my house and will have to live on the streets." The storyteller is very good at "awfulizing," which leaves you in contraction and reaction, unable to respond to the challenges of your life in a clear way.

The storyteller comes from being disconnected from Life. It comes from believing you are separated from the meadow and thus have to *do* Life rather than *be* Life. The thoughts the storyteller uses are exquisite tools for maneuvering through reality, but they are not Reality. The storyteller is not the meadow. It creates ideas about the meadow, trying to get back to it, which is only more struggle. It also has a tendency to react to Life rather than respond to it.

Now imagine an alien arriving from another planet and landing beside this meadow. He sees you in the meadow, surrounded by and permeated with clouds, struggling with Life rather than being open to it. He can see, sticking out of your clouds, feet and hands. As you run here and there around the meadow, he notices that you are hold-ing a butterfly net in one of your hands. He instinctively understands that you are trying to catch butterflies because you believe that if you capture enough of them (enough money, enough success)—and they must be the "right" ones (the right mate, the right body, the right hair, the right job)—then you will be happy.

The alien also notices that in your other hand you hold a fly swatter. Again, he instinctively understands why you are carrying this with you. He sees that you believe if you get rid of what you don't like—your big nose, your mate's irritating behaviors, or your anxiety—then you will finally feel everything is okay.

As he watches you career around the meadow, trying to get to what you like and away from what you don't like, the alien notices that all of your seeking and resisting may bring you moments of okayness, but in the long run your actions only thicken your clouds of struggle. He also sees that over and over again your desire for your life to be differ-ent than how it is results in times when you become frozen or lost in despair because you haven't been able to control your life into what you think it should be. This confuses the alien because he can clearly see that you are struggling with nothing more substantial than clouds. On top of that, he can see that you are already in the meadow of peace you are so desperately trying to find. He knows that the meadow of your natural okayness is always with you; you just don't recognize it.

The core truth being offered in this book—and I will say this over and over again because our clouds of struggle can seem so thick—is that *you are always in the meadow.* You usually don't notice it because you have been conditioned to pay attention only to the stories—the clouds—in your head.

Lasting peace is your natural state. Everything you long for and everything you truly are is to be found right here in the meadow of *this moment.* You access the meadow by simply being open to Life. Being open means having a direct experience with whatever you are experi-encing—no matter what it is—including the easy and the difficult, the joyous and the sorrowful. It is showing up for the life that you've been given rather than endlessly trying to make it be different than what it is.

14

⟨ Open to the possibility that you are in the meadow right now as you are reading this book. ⟩

REOPENING YOUR HEART

It is an amazing awakening to realize you have been chasing pleasant states your whole life and resisting the unpleasant ones, and this has never brought you the peace you long for. Rather than searching for the ultimate experience of your life, how would it feel to settle into the flow of Life enough that every experience (even the difficult) is the ultimate experience of your life? This radical acceptance opens you to the meadow of well-being.

It is your heart that knows how to be open to it all. When you are caught in the clouds of struggle, you are experiencing your life only through your mind, which clings and resists. When you thin your clouds of struggle enough, you begin to experience your life through your heart, and that is the key to remembering that the meadow is always here.

It is important to expand our definition of the heart beyond the fairly limited view that permeates our culture. Many types of wisdom—from ancient ayurvedic medicine to the modern HeartMath Institute, which helps people bridge their hearts and minds and deepen their connection with others—teach us that the core of our being is the heart. Not the physical organ, but the energy essence of the heart. Your heart is not just about feelings. It is literally an energy center that resides in your chest, and when it is open, it fills your whole being with its wisdom energy. Pull up a memory of someone you deeply care for and allow yourself to really feel how much you care. If you pay attention, you will notice that the energy in your chest opens up. Now call up a time when you were angry and reactive, and notice that the energy in your chest closes down. Pull up the first memory and allow your heart to glow again.

Your heart, rather than your mind, is the source of wisdom, healing, and love, and it is very smart. It is the heart that can feel Life, connecting with it through resonance. It knows how to include rather than exclude, to accept rather than judge, to allow rather than resist.

Your experience of Life is completely different when you learn how to feel it with your heart rather than thinking about it with your mind.

You lived with an open heart when you were very young, but like most people, you were scared out of it. In order to not continually suffer the pain of a broken heart, you ran away to your head. You were like Sleeping Beauty, pricking your finger on the spindle of your thoughts, falling asleep to the power of your heart.

But you, like Sleeping Beauty, can wake up again. As you discover how to listen to your heart and trust it again, you will discover that it is the wisest guide and friend you will ever have. Your heart is the gatekeeper for the energy of aliveness that you really are. The more closed your heart is, the more depressed you feel, and the more cut off you are from the flow of Life. The more open your heart is, the more you have access to your natural state of peace, well-being, and ease, no matter what is happening.

It is possible to live a life in which your reactive mind does not close down the wisdom of your heart, and this is what this journey we are on is all about. When you have seen through your clouds enough that your heart feels safe to open again, rather than being an object in your mind, Life becomes the subject of your heart. Every single part of you—even the so-called unacceptable parts—is woven back into your heart. Also, rather than experiencing people through your wanting and resisting mind, you experience them through your heart—even difficult people.

❦ Bring your attention to the center of your chest and breathe in and out through your heart center. If you have never done this before, imagine breathing through a little nose in the center of your chest. Now see inside your chest a tiny flame, and every time you breathe in, the flame becomes brighter. ❧

THE POWER OF COMPASSIONATE CURIOSITY

How do you rediscover the meadow of okayness rather than living in the reactions of your mind? It isn't about trying to get back to the meadow—that is just more struggle. Besides, you never left the meadow; you just think you have. The key is getting to know your clouds of struggle rather than trying to fix them, change them, or get rid of them. And the key to getting to know your clouds is learning how to be curious about what is going on in your life, both inside of you and outside, so you can see what the storyteller is doing inside your head. The more you look, the less you take these stories personally, and the easier it becomes to unhook from them. I call it "look to unhook."

Imagine being so lost in a wave of fear that your mind is whirling and you feel like there is a tight knot in your stomach. Then imagine curiosity kicking in. You notice that your belly is tight and your mind is spinning. Rather than falling into the fear, you can be with it: "This is just fear, and I can be curious about it." In that moment, rather than being lost in your mind's resistance to what you are experiencing, you have turned your attention toward what is actually happening—not an idea of it, but the living experience of it.

Reconnecting with *what is* means making contact with what you are actually experiencing before you think about it. This may not seem very powerful, but it is. Instead of being caught in fear, you have stepped back and have *related to* fear rather than being lost in it. Your ability to be aware of what is going on inside may last for just a moment before fear takes over again, but that moment matters. Learning to see what your mind is doing rather than being lost in it is an important step toward unhooking from the game of struggle.

This ability to be curious about what you are experiencing opens you to the wisdom of your heart, where you can safely meet all of your stories and the feelings they generate. If you are like most people, you are either ashamed of or afraid of the stories that make up your clouds, so you hide them deep inside. If they do make it to the surface of your awareness, you judge yourself for having them, and then you spend your energy ignoring them or getting rid of them. But thoughts are just like people. They react when they are judged, and they let go when they are listened to.

You can learn how to bring compassionate curiosity to all of the stories in your head. The more you bring the light of your compassionate attention to the stories you have been caught in most of your life, the more they thin, like clouds touched by the warmth of the sun. And as the clouds thin, it's as if a doorway opens through which you can once again experience the meadow, which is the place where everything is okay, no matter what is happening in your life.

❧ Take a moment to listen to Life again. Notice that the sounds are different than when you listened a few pages ago. In these few moments you are using your mind to be curious about Life rather than just thinking about it. ❧

WHAT'S IN THE WAY *IS* THE WAY

The more you are curious about what you are experiencing, rather than trying to change it, the more you discover an amazing truth: you naturally know how to partner with Life instead of always trying to change it. You also see that no object, person, or experience will ever bring you the deep and lasting peace that comes from simply being open to Life. You then become less interested in trying to create your reality and more willing to show up for Life as it unfolds.

As your ability to be curious increases, it becomes evident that Life is *for* you. It is very difficult, if not impossible, to see this truth when you are caught in the clouds of struggle. We will be exploring this truth in more depth toward the end of the book, but know that the more your clouds thin, the more you can see that Life is trustable. It is not always likable, but what's in the way *is* the way, and it can be trusted. Trust does not mean trusting that you will get what you *want*. It means understanding you will get what you *need* in order to come out of the clouds of struggle. So trust doesn't just trust the easy, it also trusts the difficult. Trust knows that the challenges of your life are for you. They are the yellow highlighter of Life showing you the clouds of your reactive mind so that you can thin them with the sunlight of your own compassionate attention and thus rediscover the meadow of this moment.

As compassionate curiosity develops inside of you and brings you to your natural state of trust, you will be able to relax and allow Life to flow through you rather than resisting or trying to hold on to it. Your life then becomes an adventure, and every moment is an invitation to either engage with the joy of being fully alive or stay lost in your stories of struggle. The more your clouds thin, the more your energy opens up. The more you open up, the more you connect with Life.

❀ Let go of all that we have been exploring here and use whatever senses are calling to you to make direct contact with Life. Hear it, see it, touch it, feel it coursing through your body. This is a brand-new moment in your life. You have never experienced this moment before and never will again. The quality of light is different; the sensations in your body are different; even the sounds you are hearing are brand new. There is an intelligent flow going on here, a flow that you can consciously feel through the wisdom of your heart. Stay with this flow as long as it interests you, whether it is for two seconds or ten minutes. ❀

KEY POINTS

At the end of each chapter in this book there is a list of the chapter's main points, along with space for you to write down what ideas touched you most. This list will be helpful in keeping in the forefront of your awareness the shifts of perception that are happening as you go through the Remembering process.

- No matter what your mind says, everything is and always will be okay.

- You have a storyteller in your head that talks all day long and doesn't recognize this okayness.

- The storyteller tries to do Life rather than being open to it.

- Everything you long for and everything you truly are is always right here, right now.

- The doorway to freedom comes from your willingness to be curious about your own clouds of struggle.

- The more you bring the light of your compassionate attention to the stories you have been caught in, the more they thin, just like clouds thin when touched by the sun's warmth.

- Life is completely different when you learn how to feel your way with your heart rather than thinking about it with your mind.

- Life is trustable. It is not always likable, but what's in the way *is* the way.

- This trust is not trusting that you will get what you *want*. Trust understands that you'll get what you *need* in order to come out of the clouds of struggle.

- The challenges of your life are for you. They are the yellow highlighter of Life showing you the clouds of your reactive mind so that you can thin them with the sunlight of your own attention and thus rediscover the meadow of this moment.

-

-

-

REMEMBERING   Week 1
This week's Remembering Statement:
Right now, this is Life, and it's okay.
Your own statement:

Remembering Session

Let us now strengthen the muscle of your attention so you can discover how to be present for your own experience. Find a comfortable spot where you won't be interrupted by people, phones, or pets. We will start by relaxing the chronic holding in your body, and then we will bring your attention to the circle of your breath. Your breath is the mother rhythm of Life, and it has been with you since the moment you were born. And it is always here no matter what is happening in your life.

❊ Begin by closing your eyes and taking a moment to recognize that all of the millions of moments of your life have brought you to this unique moment. You are not watching television, taking a shower, or eating your breakfast. You are sitting with your eyes closed, with the intention to become curious about what you are experiencing right now. Notice what you can notice about this moment of your life.

On the next in-breath, tighten your muscles. Tighten, tighten, tighten. Then slowly—very slowly—relax everything on your out-breath as you say the great sound of letting go: *Ahh!* Feel the deliciousness of deeply letting go, coupled with the power of *Ahh.* (If you are in a place where it's uncomfortable to make sounds, say *Ahh!* silently to yourself.) Play with this sound, as there are many different ways you can express it.

This act of tension and release melts the chronic holding that shows up in your body and mind all day long. Repeat for at least three breaths.

Now allow your breath to be as it wants to be, and be curious about how different an in-breath is from an out-breath. An in-breath lifts and opens you up from the inside. As it comes to its end, it turns, becoming the relaxation and letting go of the out-breath, a much different experience than an in-breath. Then comes a pause, then another in-breath fills you up.

To remind yourself that you are riding the waves of your breath, say silently to yourself, "In . . . out. Deep . . . slow." Say *in* on the in-breath and *out* on the out-breath. Say *deep* on the next in-breath and *slow* on the next out-breath. As you are learning to add these words to your breath, it can be helpful to write them on a card that you keep beside you. Leave space for two more pairs of words; we will add them in the coming Remembering Sessions.

There is no need to judge every time you drift off into your storyteller again. You have been paying attention to your thoughts for most of your life. Simply bring your attention back to being curious about the circle of your breath and these calming, focusing words. Stay with this as long as it interests you.

At the end, open your attention to include your whole body and notice what is different now that you have given yourself the healing of your own attention.

When you are ready, open your eyes. ⸙

Abbreviated Version

⸙ Close your eyes and dip the finger of your attention into the river of your experience, noticing what it is like to be you right now.

For at least three breaths, tighten your muscles on your in-breath. Then slowly—very slowly—relax everything on your out-breath as you say the great sound of letting go, *Ahh!*

Now be curious about the circle of your breath as you say silently to yourself, "In . . . out. Deep . . . slow."

Every time you drift off into your thoughts again, without judgment, bring your attention back to the circle of your breath and the calming, focusing words. Stay with the breath and the words as long as you are interested.

At the end, expand your awareness and be curious about what is happening inside of you after a few minutes of conscious breathing.

When you are ready, open your eyes. ❦

2

Getting to Know the Meadow

When you are identified with the storyteller in your head, which is the voice of your clouds of struggle, you live from a tight and small place that's disconnected from your heart, disconnected from the amazing beauty and mystery of Life. To unhook from your storyteller is to become spacious and open—the opposite of the world of low-grade struggle that you are accustomed to. In unhooking, you discover how to use your mind for the exquisite tool it is rather than letting it be in charge. Let us take a few minutes to explore the amazing creativity of Life in order to get a feel for what it is like to unhook, so that you can connect with the spaciousness and openness that is the meadow of well-being within you.

Imagine being transported to the moon—brown dust and rock. Now as you look at Earth before you, be stunned by how the creativity of Life was able to explode into a mind-boggling array of forms and colors—all the way from jungles filled with colorful parrots, to pristine icebergs floating majestically in silent waters, to miles and miles of coral beds, to waves of grass dancing in the wind, to herds of baby seals with their liquid-brown eyes.

This universe where you find yourself has been unfolding for billions of years, birthing stars, exploding stars, and then creating out of stardust this magical and mysterious planet we call home. If you start from the beginning and fast-forward, watching the unfolding of Life like a movie, you will see that forms—a planet, a mountain, a ladybug, a human being—continuously appear and disappear.

In the process of all this appearing and disappearing, you have shown up. You have been given the gift of experiencing a tiny slice of this 13.8-billion-year process. What a valuable gift that is! Imagine that there is a single turtle in all the seas of the world, and that turtle surfaces from the water only once every hundred years. Now imagine there is also a single golden hoop floating on the seas, tossed this way and that by the winds and currents. How often would the turtle, on its once-a-century visit to the surface, put its head through the golden hoop? It has been said that to be given a human life is just as rare as that happening.

For a moment, allow your whole being to open into the joy of that miracle. Life has been evolving for billions of years before you arrived, and it will continue long after you depart. For a few precious years you get to experience this constantly unfolding river of Life. The doorway back into consciously connecting with Life is this moment. This is the only moment that matters in your whole life. This moment in which you are reading this book is the place where you can rediscover all of the joy, the creativity, and the Love that is at the heart of Life.

❦ Dip the finger of your attention into the river of your experience by lifting your eyes and simply open to your life as it is right now. See it. Hear it. Fully experience it. This moment is uniquely different from any other moment of your life. ❧

Now realize that you have missed the full experience of Life most of your life. You, like most people, withdrew from Life when you were very young, crawling into a conceptual world that keeps on churning out ideas about Life. But rarely, if ever, did you allow yourself to experience the real thing. Before you became immersed in a conceptual world, when you saw a cat, you really saw it; you really experienced the cat as a unique and amazing creation of Life. As you became entranced with the world of thought, you stopped fully experiencing

Life. Instead, you experienced your ideas about it. As a Zen teacher once said, "No matter how many times you say the word *water*, it will never be wet." In other words, no matter how much you think about Life, it isn't the same as truly experiencing it.

So you walk around caught in your thoughts, homesick for a direct experience of Life. You long for it, but you are also afraid of it. You retreated into the world of your mind when you were young because Life was big and unpredictable and scary. Your mind said, "Let's figure out how to control Life, and then we will be safe." So you have occupied your time trying to *do* Life and do it right, not realizing that in the process, you turned into a human "doing" rather than a human being, trading the direct experience of Life for the illusion of control.

You stay caught in your mind, afraid of becoming fully who you are because you are not quite sure what that would look like. But I can assure you that seeing through your clouds and coming back to Life is the safest thing you will ever do, for it is all about coming home. What that looks and feels like will become clearer as we explore the qualities of your essence and you learn the skills needed to relate to your clouds rather than from them.

THE QUALITIES OF THE MEADOW

On our adventure together, we are exploring, step by step, how to see through the clouds of your mind so you can clear a pathway back into the meadow of well-being within you. Before we start clearing your clouds of struggle, however, it is important to take a look at how you will experience Life living from the meadow. We need to do this because you were so conditioned to be afraid of Life when you were very young that if you don't recognize the safety and the joy of being open to Life, you will resist what is being offered here.

There are five core qualities that are the essence of the meadow, and as you relearn how to open into Life, you will live from these qualities. They are:

- flow
- spaciousness

- light
- Love
- stillness

These qualities have always been within you; they are with you right now as you are reading this book. But you haven't noticed them because they have been covered over by the clouds of struggle. So you don't really need to find them. All you need to do is learn how to thin your clouds of struggle, and there they are.

As we explore these five core qualities, it is important to recognize that there is violence and chaos in Life. There is also death; everything in Life appears for a time and then recedes back into mystery. In the meadow there is no resistance to violence, chaos, or death. The five qualities of the meadow embrace these aspects of Life rather than fighting or resisting them. True joy comes when we can be with what is—no matter what is! And if you look closely, you will see that new life is born from all of these five qualities.

Flow

Everywhere you look, Life flows. Rivers flow from the mountains to the sea, clouds flow across the sky, oceans flow in waves and tides. As air flows around this planet on the jet streams, wind dances through the trees. Blood flows throughout your body due to the pulsing of your heart; at the same time, information flows along your network of nerves.

In the great circle of Life, flow shows up in the dance of day and night and changes from one season into the next. Death is also a part of this flow. Life arises out of mystery, expressing itself in an amazing variety of forms, and each and every one will dissolve back into mystery. Even the invisible world flows. Light shows up as waves of energy, and each color is a wave with a different frequency. Sound is simply waves of vibration touching your eardrum.

Imagine the meadow a hundred years ago and fast-forward the unfolding of this little piece of the planet. You will see that over and over again day flows into night and back again. Clouds come and go; sounds arise and pass away. Winter flows into spring, plants appear and dissolve, animals are born and die. Everything in the meadow is about flow. Now expand your view, and see this flow happening everywhere on our planet.

If you look closely, you will also see that Intelligence permeates the flow of Life. This Intelligence is so creative that you begin as just one cell, too small to see with the naked eye, then it unfolds into trillions of cells that all work together without a thought from you. When was the last time you had to work to get your hair to grow or your stomach to digest your food or your heart to beat? This Intelligence is also so smart that it knows which tiny seed will turn into a sequoia tree and which will grow into a carrot. It is the Intelligence within the flow of Life that tells each seed what it will become.

The only things in all of creation that don't flow are the clouds of struggle in our minds.

These clouds create the illusion that there is a "me" in here and there is Life out there. The mind believes itself to be separate from the flow of Life and believes that its job is to control everything. It lives from fixed positions: good/bad, right/wrong, liking/disliking. As long as you see yourself as separate, you will view Life as a potential threat and withdraw from the flow of Life into the clouds in your mind.

All you have to do is look at the human condition to see how much suffering our belief in separation creates. Most human beings live in a constant, low-grade struggle inside themselves. This struggle eventually shows up as all the suffering on this planet: greed, fear, hatred, despair, violence, loneliness. This belief in our separation from Life gets stronger as we grow older, which only further cuts us off from the flow of Life. And this separation from Life allows us to act in ways that hurt ourselves and others.

What would it be like to relax again into the flow of Life? Rather than trying to control Life, your intent is to open to its flow. You have known what it is like to be this intimately engaged with Life. Remember falling in love? There is lightness in your step, vibrancy in your being, and no need to have things be any different than they are. Why do you feel this way? Because love has opened you again to Life. This is why most people are so addicted to love. It is one of the few experiences that can penetrate the clouds of struggle, inviting you simply to be fully here with Life. But as you have probably discovered, this kind of love doesn't last. Your clouds reconfigure, and your life narrows once again to a chronic game of struggle.

It is possible to live from the ease that comes from discovering how to be open to the flow of Life. To open again, it is important to recognize that Life is an intelligent flow. You may not always understand or like it, but you can trust it. You can wake up every morning with a willingness to show up for the great adventure called Life. The key is to discover how to stay open to whatever Life is bringing you. As you do, you will come to the place where it doesn't matter whether you are falling in love, dying, feeling nauseated or anxious, witnessing a beautiful sunset, having a challenging conversation with your boss, or joyfully watching kittens. It is all just Life passing through the spaciousness of who you truly are.

To enter the flow of Life by being open to this moment—no matter what it is bringing you—is to learn how to fully feel, but not hold on to, wonderful states and not shut down and push the difficult ones away. Life will continue to give you extremes of experience—joyful and sorrowful, easy and challenging, beautiful and unappealing. If your happiness is dependent on Life being a particular way, it is a given that the flow of Life will eventually dissolve the circumstances that are bringing you happiness, just like the tide washes away your writing in the sand. And if you are afraid of the pains and discomforts of Life, you will resist them, turning them into suffering.

Joy, your natural state, isn't dependent on Life being any particular way. Joy comes from the ability to be fully engaged with the flow of Life exactly as it is appearing—no matter what that is—and allowing Life to pass through you rather than always trying to make it be a certain way. Peace comes when you discover that you don't have to tighten around the difficult or hold on to the beautiful. As Pema Chödrön, an internationally known author and Buddhist nun, says in her 2009 book *Taking the Leap,* "Peace isn't an experience free of challenges, free of rough and smooth, it's an experience that's expansive enough to include all that arises without feeling threatened."

⊰ Take a moment to lift your eyes from the book and see with new eyes. Everything you see is Life flowing, and in that flow, everything in the space you are in has changed since you started reading. It may not look like it's changed, but it is the truth. The sounds around you have changed; your body is a few minutes older. If you are inside, the rug and the lamps are a little bit closer to eventually going to the garbage dump, and if you are outside, everything in nature has altered with the flow of time. This all happens so slowly that we don't usually notice it, but it is happening nonetheless. ⊱

Spaciousness

The second quality of Life that permeates the meadow is spaciousness. If you look carefully, you will see that Life loves space. Right now, as you are reading this book, you are sitting on a planet that is dancing through vast oceans of space. For heaven's sake, it is 24.8 trillion miles to the closest star! Then there are stars that are billions of times farther away than that. Can you even begin to imagine how much space that is? And this is all happening in a universe that seems to have no end.

Now let's go in the other direction—into your body. It is estimated that you are made up of anywhere from 70 to 100 trillion cells, and each of those is composed of around 100 trillion atoms. If you blow up one of those atoms to be the size of a major-league baseball field, the nucleus would be a grain of sand in the middle of the field, and the electrons would be dancing around the outside of the stadium. So even atoms are mainly made up of space, and because you are made up of atoms, you are space too. You probably experience yourself as solid, but science says that is just a trick of perception. Space is the truth of your being.

When lost in your clouds, you live in the tight and narrow space of your mind. When you are open to this moment, spaciousness permeates your body, mind, and heart. Imagine a morning that you get up and ignore the to-do list. Instead, you luxuriate in bed. You linger at breakfast, and you follow your heart as to how the day will unfold.

This is a day in which you feel the deliciousness of spaciousness. You unhook from the mental pressure of having to do something, and instead you enjoy Life. This is your natural state, and it can be accessed no matter what is happening in your life. To live from spaciousness doesn't mean that you will want to disengage from your life. It means that you won't be fighting with it anymore.

You can also unhook emotionally to give yourself the gift of space. Imagine a time when you did something that you previously judged yourself for. This time, instead of getting caught in self-judgment, you touch yourself with your own heart, accepting yourself as you are. You give yourself the space to be human, and it feels so much better than being lost in the tightness of self-judgment. Or think of a time when your friend or mate acted in a way that upset you. Imagine instead that you decided not to take it personally and you let your reaction go. In both of these situations, you probably took a deeper breath because you moved from the tightness of reaction to the openness of acceptance.

To experience how tight and small you usually are, think about being frustrated at the length of a stoplight. That frustration may not seem like much tightness, but where is the joy? Then think of a time when you had a headache and you desperately wanted it to go away. Can you feel that when you resist the pain, the tightness in your head gets stronger and affects not only the headache but also your whole body?

Now let's go in the opposite direction. Recall a time when you were delightfully surprised by Life; or remember when a major project was completed, and it felt like a huge weight had been lifted off of your shoulders. Can you feel how your energy expands inside of you? When you are caught in the clouds in your mind, everything becomes contracted. The thicker the clouds, the smaller and tighter you become. When you stay open to Life, you are more spacious, so energy flows freely through you, allowing you to experience the pure joy of being alive.

Your birthright is to be the opposite of tight and small. Your natural state is openness, and it is only your conditioning that causes you to tighten and live small. It is possible to open again and live in spaciousness, even if your mind is caught in judgment, your heart is sad, and your life is overwhelming. How can that be? Because your natural state is to be the meadow, and from the meadow you can learn how to allow any reaction to simply to pass through the spaciousness of your being.

> ❦ Take a moment and recognize that right now as you are sitting here, you are completely surrounded by stars. They are above you, below you, to the left and to the right of you. These stars are all dancing together, and our beautiful planet is a part of this celestial dance. If your mind gets scared by the immensity of it all, hold its hand and invite it for just a few moments to become expansive and open. Stay with this feeling, allowing yourself to recognize how delicious it is to experience this spaciousness. ❧

Light

As you reconnect with space and flow, you can know the third aspect of the meadow: light. In the Creation story at the very beginning of the Bible, it says, "And God said, let there be light!" And according to the Book of Genesis, this statement comes before the creation of the sun and stars. We think of light as coming from the sun, but the leading edge of science is now saying that *everything* is made out of light. David Bohm, the grandfather of quantum physics, once said that matter is just frozen light.

In his book *The Planetary Mind*, Arne Wyller reports, "Almost all particles in the Universe are those of light." He goes on to say, "Light is a vital ingredient in all atoms." Since everything is made of atoms, it follows that everything—a cat, a tree, a rock, the human body—is made of light.

We have all met people whose eyes twinkle and whose presence radiates a sense of warmth. We often say they glow. That is what you begin to see when you rediscover the meadow of well-being within you and all around you. Everything shines from within, radiating the energy of its presence. You may not see this, but when you get quiet enough, you can feel it.

Most of the time, you dim the radiance of your being by only paying attention to the clouds in your mind. This is true of all human beings: most of us have dimmed our light. The more you are lost in the problem factory of your mind, the thicker the clouds are in and around your head, cutting you off from the radiance of your body and the pure joy of being alive. No matter how thick your clouds become, however, they never stop the truth of your radiance. And it is possible to shine again like you did when you were young.

Take a moment to shake one of your hands vigorously. Now stop shaking, close your eyes, and feel your hand. There is the flow of energy—the tingles, the aliveness. This is an artificial way to experience what it feels like when your energy is open and spacious. It feels good. It feels alive.

The ecstatic Persian poet Hafiz spoke directly to what we are talking about in his poem "My Brilliant Image," as translated by Daniel Ladinsky in his book *I Heard God Laughing:*

One day the sun admitted,

I am just a shadow.
I wish I could show you
The Infinite Incandescence (Tej)

That has cast my brilliant image!

I wish I could show you,
When you are lonely or in darkness,

The Astonishing Light

Of your own Being!

"The Astonishing Light / Of your own Being"—what a wonderful phrase! You have so much energy within you that wants to be freed from the game of struggle so it can expand and dance, and when energy is free to flow, it shines. This is what you are hungry for—your own radiance. It's no accident that when a great burden has been lifted or you feel very happy, you often say, "I feel so light!" It is also no coincidence that the word *delight* means "of the light." Even pictures of saints point to what we are talking about. The reason most saints are painted with halos around their heads is because they broke free from the clouds of struggle so their light could shine, and people recognized this light.

There is a saying, often attributed to Plato, that says: "We can easily forgive a child who is afraid of the dark; the real tragedy of life is when men are afraid of the light." We are all afraid of our own light. You need to forgive yourself for being so afraid of opening to Life. You were scared out of it when you were very young. But even though you have been afraid, you can learn the safety of opening again. You can, to paraphrase Jesus, learn not to hide your light under the bushel of your clouds. This is the greatest gift you can give to humanity—to shine from within because you are open to Life. Carl Jung said, "As far as we can discern, the sole purpose of human existence is to kindle a light in the darkness of mere being." You too can shine and know the joy of your own radiance.

✦ Take a moment and shake your hand again. When you stop, bring your attention to your hand and feel the tingles. As they fade away, expand your attention and feel the subtle tingles all over your body that come from the energy of Life. If they are hard to find, put your attention a foot away from your body and then slowly bring it closer. Notice the difference between the space around you and the actual experience of the energy of your body. That energy wants to expand and glow in joy. ✦

Love

When you rediscover the spaciousness of being open again to the great flow of Life—when you feel energy moving through you rather than trying to control it—you begin to recognize that the word that best describes this movement of light is *Love*. There is great truth in the song title "Love Makes the World Go 'Round." It not only makes it go around, it permeates absolutely everything.

In Greek, there are four words for love: *eros* (romantic love), *philia* (the love of friendship), *storge* (the love of family), and *agape* (universal or unconditional love). In English, we are hampered by having only one word for love, so I am capitalizing the word *Love* to point to the truth that Love (agape) is the essence of Life.

Eben Alexander, a neurosurgeon and author of the bestselling book *Proof of Heaven,* wrote about what happened while he was in a seven-day coma from spinal meningitis. When asked what was the core of what he experienced while he was out of his body, he said, "Love is, without a doubt, the basis of everything. . . . This is the reality of realities, the incomprehensibly glorious truth of truths that lives and breathes at the core of everything that exists or will ever exist, and no remotely accurate understanding of who and what we are can be achieved by anyone who does not know it, and embody it in all of their actions."

Brian Swimme, an author and evolutionary cosmologist, calls this essence at the heart of Life "allurement." This force of attraction can be seen from the very beginning of our universe. The "stuff" that arose out of the Big Bang followed the call of attraction and came together into communities we call atoms. Then these atoms were drawn together into communities called molecules. Then the molecules were so attracted to one another they came together into communities called cells, and then cells followed the call of allurement and became multicellular beings.

This attracting force at the heart of Life then showed up in the mating dance of insects and animals, and in their daily life as well. In Charles Darwin's book *The Descent of Man,* he mentions "survival of the fittest" only twice, but he mentions "love" ninety-five times when referring to the behavior of the creatures he was observing. He also talks about conciliation and cooperation being the most significant mode of behavior among them all.

This urge to connect at the heart of Life is all about Love. The great mystics of the world have all agreed that when you come out of the clouds in your mind, what you recognize and fully become is Love. And it is this Love, this allurement, this urge to connect, that brings together all things, whether it is subatomic particles or human beings or solar systems.

Every cell in your being is filled with this Love, and it fuels almost everything you do. But you have been conditioned to search for it outside of yourself, leading inevitably to the often endless, and mostly unsatisfying, search for somebody to love you. What would happen if you recognized that Love is right here, right now? What would happen if you realized that Love is not something you need to find, but who you already are?

Love is what constitutes absolutely everything. The more your heart opens, the more you can feel the energy of Love that animates everything: trees, rocks, birds, clouds, your dog, and even the sun. Hafiz, who was truly awake to this Love that is at the heart of Life, speaks to this truth in his poem "The Sun Never Says," translated by Daniel Ladinsky in his book *The Gift:*

Even
After
All this time
The sun never says to the earth,

"You owe
Me."

Look
What happens
With a love like that,
It lights the
Whole
Sky.

Even the sun is an expression of the Love at the heart of Life, endlessly giving forth its light. In the sun's giving, the entire earth thrives. In learning how to live from your heart, you become as lit up as the sun, giving forth the warm, radiant energy of Love as you move through your day. Just as atoms, molecules, and cells were drawn together into greater communities, you will draw others into the community of the heart. It is the heart that recognizes we are all unique expressions of the Love that is the essence of Life, and it is the heart that will wake us up to the truth that we are all in this together, floating on a tiny, blue-green jewel of a planet that is dancing through vast oceans of space.

❦ Gently place your hand over your heart and contemplate the possibility that you are the lover you have been waiting for. ❧

Stillness

Look out at the world and see this dance that has been going on for eons—things arising and passing away—mosquitoes, dinosaurs, your great-grandparents, mountains, and even stars. Everything in this dance of Life appears and then eventually disappears. This constant movement of Life extends all the way out to the dance of galaxies and all the way within to electrons dancing around the nucleus of every single atom of your body. But that is only half of it. All of this movement arises out of a vast stillness—a stillness that births all the varied forms of Life.

Father Thomas Keating, a Trappist monk and a founder of the Centering Prayer movement, wrote in *Invitation to Love*, "Silence is God's first language; everything else is a poor translation." If you find a quiet place to sit in nature and allow your mind to quiet down, you can feel the stillness and silence out of which all form arises and into which it returns in the ongoing cycles of birth and death.

This stillness is also within you. Eckhart Tolle, author of *Stillness Speaks*, says, "Your innermost sense of self, of who you are, is inseparable from stillness." Yet most people know nothing of this stillness within. They have been conditioned not to listen. Instead they are so busy running here and there that it is almost impossible for them to simply become quiet and allow their thoughts to settle so that they can recognize this stillness and be nourished by its presence. It is possible, even in the midst of a busy life, to rest in stillness, which opens you up to a deep and passionate listening to Life.

Even more than longing for the joy of opening to the great flow of Life, you are homesick for this stillness. Because you were not trained to notice your own stillness, you can't tap into its wisdom. It is as if you have been at a beautiful outdoor symphony your whole life, but one noisy person (your busy mind) keeps distracting your attention from the symphony of your own stillness.

This stillness is not something you can search for. Searching for it is just more conflict—more trying to have your experience be different than what it is. The stillness at the core of your being is the absence of conflict, so trying to find it will only close the door to the stillness. In your willingness just to be curious about what is happening inside of you, the struggling self naturally calms down enough for stillness to reveal itself.

It is not an empty stillness you discover as you turn your attention within. It is full and rich, permeated with the Love and Intelligence at the heart of Life. It is the source of "the still, small voice" that is always with you. It is the place where you discover you are not alone. The presence of stillness, the knowing of stillness, the Love that is inherent in the stillness is always with you. When you recognize this, you are then able to partner with the wisdom of Life.

Being connected to stillness doesn't mean that you sit beside the road of Life, just resting in quiet and peace. In fact, the exact opposite is true. You become more fully engaged with Life, and your responses arise out of this stillness, rather than coming from the busy mind that believes itself to be separate from Life.

⸙ For a few moments, close your eyes and watch
how busy your mind is. Know that underneath all of
that noise is a field of deep stillness. This stillness is
always with you, and you can discover how to rest in
its embrace. ⸙

As you drink in these five qualities that are at the core of who you truly are, it is important to recognize that they are here with you right now. You may not notice them, but they are always with you no matter what is happening in your life. As you see through your clouds of struggle, you begin to recognize these qualities and to live from them, and this brings you to the okayness we explored in the last chapter.

The rest of the book is about accessing these five qualities that make up the meadow. You won't be reconnecting with them by trying to find them. That just creates more struggle. Instead, you will learn how to see through the clouds in your mind so they can thin, and you can discover the joy of living from these five qualities of the meadow rather than from your busy, controlling mind. In doing so, you will discover that the qualities of the meadow are the qualities of your very being.

KEY POINTS

- When you live in the clouds in your head, you live tight and small—disconnected from your heart, disconnected from the amazing beauty and mystery of Life.

- Life has been evolving for billions of years before you arrived, and it will continue long after you depart. For a few precious years, you get to experience this constantly unfolding river of Life.

- The five qualities that are the essence of the meadow—flow, spaciousness, light, Love, and stillness—have always been with you, but you haven't noticed them because they have been covered over by the clouds of struggle.

- As your clouds clear, you begin to recognize the five qualities and to live from them. This brings you to the okayness that is your natural state.

- To enter the flow of Life by being open to this moment—no matter what it is bringing you—is to learn how not to hold on to wonderful states or push the difficult ones away.

• To come out of your clouds of struggle is to become spacious and open—the opposite of the world of low-grade struggle that you are used to.

• You have so much energy within you that wants to be let out of the prison of struggle so it can expand and dance and shine. This is what you are hungry for—your own radiance.

• Love is the basis of everything.

• All of Life arises out of a vast stillness, and this stillness is the essence of who you really are. It is full and rich, permeated with the Love and Intelligence at the heart of Life.

• You can't try to find the five qualities. That just creates more struggle. Instead, you can get to know your clouds so they can thin, and the five qualities will reveal themselves.

•

•

•

REMEMBERING   Week 2
This week's Remembering Statement:
The meadow is here right now or _____ *is here right now.*
(Name one: flow, spaciousness, light, Love, stillness.)
Your own statement:

Remembering Session

This week we are exploring a powerful way to calm down the stories of struggle that make up the clouds in your mind. This way, it will become easier to reconnect with the five qualities of the meadow. You'll do this by the simple act of deepening your breath through focusing on the out-breath. If you are timing your session, allow about six minutes. If time is not an issue, stay with each step as long as your curiosity is engaged.

Let's begin:

❦ Close your eyes and dip the finger of your attention into the river of your experience, noticing what it is like to be you right now.

For at least three breaths, tighten your muscles on your in-breath and then very slowly relax everything on your out-breath as you say the great sound of letting go: *Ahh!*

Bring your attention to the circle of your breath.

To deepen your out-breath, first imagine a lit candle floating in the air in front of you. Breathe in through your nostrils and then gently blow out through your mouth, imagining you are blowing out this candle. As you become comfortable with this rhythm, allow yourself to enjoy the deliciousness of a long, slow out-breath.

As you become comfortable with a longer out-breath, you can let go of the candle image and breathe in and out through your nostrils, continuing to enjoy a long, slow out-breath. Say silently to yourself on the rhythm of your breath, "In . . . out. Deep . . . slow." Stay with this circle of breath as long as it interests you.

Whenever you notice that you are no longer paying attention to the circle of your breath, no judgment. Simply bring your attention back.

For a few moments before you close, open your attention to include your whole body, and notice what is different now that you have given yourself the gift of your own attention.

When you are ready, open your eyes. ⸘

Abbreviated Version

⸘ Close your eyes and dip the finger of your attention into the river of your experience, noticing what it is like to be you right now.

For at least three in-breaths, tighten your muscles, and then very slowly relax everything on your out-breath as you say the great sound of letting go: *Ahh!*

Bring your attention to the circle of your breath.

Imagining there is a lit candle in front of you, breathe in through your nostrils, and then blow out the candle, enjoying a long, slow out-breath.

When you are ready, let go of the candle image and breathe in and out through your nostrils, as you say to yourself on the rhythm of your breath, "In . . . out. Deep . . . slow."

When you notice that you are no longer paying attention to your breath, simply bring your attention back to it, with no judgment.

For a few moments at the end, open your attention to include your whole body, and notice what is different now that you have given yourself the gift of your own attention.

When you are ready, open your eyes. ⊁

3

Fear—It's Nothing to Be Afraid Of

Picture the meadow in your imagination, and recognize that the flow, spaciousness, light, Love, and stillness that permeate the meadow are inside of you right now. These five qualities make up your natural state, and there is a deep longing in you to know and live from them.

Now see yourself standing in the meadow. You always are in the meadow, but you don't recognize it because your head is surrounded and filled by the clouds of struggle you were conditioned into when you were young.

Now see the clouds dissipating and feel yourself fully present with the light, Love, flow, spaciousness, and stillness of the meadow. Experience the joy of that!

To reopen your heart and remember that you are always in the meadow, you need to thin the clouds of struggle. The way you do this is by getting to know your storyteller, which is the voice of your clouds of struggle. So the next step is to become curious about what stories are happening in your head—without getting lost in them. The doorway to freedom opens when you can see what your storyteller is doing rather than being identified with its stories.

Imagine that you are sitting in a movie theater, watching your life on the big screen as the storyteller in your head is narrating. Most of the time you aren't aware of what your storyteller is saying; you just tumble from one thought to another all day long. But now, as you watch the experiences of your life emerging on the screen and hear your storyteller's running commentary in your head, you are bound to notice how much your storyteller struggles with almost everything. It struggles with big things and little things. It is often upset about aspects of your body, from the color of your hair to a life-threatening disease. And it is often frustrated by what other people are doing, from how they are driving to how they are supervising your work.

True, the storyteller isn't always struggling. If it gets what it wants, it can feel quite good. You have the new iPad, your favorite contestant on the reality show is ahead of everybody else, or somebody you like a lot says, "I love you." But from your vantage point in front of the screen, you can see clearly how this kind of happiness is only there as long as things are going the way the storyteller wants them to go. If the iPad gets stolen or you don't have enough money to buy the upgraded version, if your favorite contestant is voted off the show, or if your partner's behavior upsets you, the storyteller gets upset and starts to struggle with what is. You can then see the scenes on the movie screen turning into struggle again.

Watching carefully, you will see that the storyteller inside of your head swings from liking to disliking all day long. It likes the weather, or it doesn't. It likes your mate, or it is frustrated with him/her. It likes the chocolate cookies but only until you eat too many, and then it doesn't like itself. It likes when your life is very busy and is scared when not enough is going on, or vice versa. It likes when the stoplight is long enough for you to put on makeup. It dislikes the length of the stoplight when you may be late to work. Once you see this pendulum inside of you that swings between liking and disliking all day long, you recognize how exhausting this swing is.

What if on the armrest of your theater seat there were a bunch of buttons that allowed you to change not only what you were thinking and feeling, but other people's behavior as well? This is one of the favorite strategies of the storyteller. It says that if you could just change your mate or your boss or your friends or your child, making them be the way you think they should be, then everything would be okay (or would it?).

You do this same thing with yourself. It is very seductive to feel that if you just made yourself different, then you would finally know peace. You can watch yourself up there on the screen doing affirmations, promising you will never be compulsive again, or trying to think positive thoughts. But you can also see that these may help only for a period of time, and then the struggling storyteller takes over again. So back to the buttons you go, becoming frustrated and despairing that you haven't been able to get yourself together. No wonder most people don't live from pure joy!

❮ Right now, step out of the movie theater of your mind and dip the finger of your attention into the river of your experience, keeping your attention fluid and open. You may notice the sounds around you, a slight headache, a feeling of peace, a tickle on your back, or resistance to doing this exercise. Simply notice what you notice when you turn your attention to Life. Little moments like this matter. Just as drops of water create the oceans, moments of being fully open to Life help thin your clouds, so you can rediscover the meadow that is always within you right here, right now. ❯

YOUR CHILDHOOD AND FEAR

What fuels the struggles of the storyteller in our heads? There is one simple word that sums it all up: *fear.* Most people, most of the time, are caught in a low-grade fear that can flare into anxiousness, insecurity, and even full-blown terror. Let us now get to know fear, because within this knowing lies the possibility of not being controlled by fear.

It is true that fear is a part of Life. Think about stepping off the curb and hearing the sound of a truck barreling toward you. Without a thought, you leap back in fear. That kind of fear is necessary for survival, but it is only about 1 percent of the fear you experience. Most of what you experience is psychological fear. It is the stories of fear that move through your mind all the time.

Sometimes there are big fears, like the fear of illness and death. Sometimes there are smaller ones like "Will my pants fit?" Whether fear shows up as the slow drip of insecurity or visits you in the middle of the night and shakes you to your core, fear is always narrating your world. You are so enamored by fear's need to make sure the next thing goes right that you can't really enjoy Life.

It wasn't always that way. When you were very young, you knew instinctual fear: you startled at the sound of a loud noise or were overwhelmed by things you experienced when your parents left you alone. These clouds of fear would pass through you, leaving hardly a trace. But it didn't take long before you began to know psychological fear. When you were small, the world was big and scary. People around you were like giants—you barely came up to their knees. These big, sometimes scary giants had crawled into their clouds of struggle a long time ago, and they often acted in ways that were confusing and frightening.

Some of us had parents with clouds full of lightning and thunder. Most of us had parents whose clouds were just foggy. They had left themselves for the world of their minds when they were growing up. Living in their clouds of struggle, they didn't know how to fully connect with their children.

In their disconnection, all parents give their children two core wounds: invasion and abandonment. Invasion can range from a parent who constantly denies your feelings to one who is sexually abusive. Abandonment can vary from an overly busy parent who doesn't have time for the child, to one who actually walks out and never comes back. So whether your parents' clouds were stormy or foggy—whether your parents were mildly neglectful or majorly abusive—fear was generated inside of you as you tried to make sense of what was going on.

❦ On your movie-theater seat armrest is a button that rewinds the movie to a day in your childhood before you were six. Push that button. Allow yourself to view an experience with your parent or parents that scared you. Remember, you can also hear what your storyteller is saying during this experience. Can you feel its fear?

Know you had many moments such as this when you were growing up, and as you listen to what is going on inside of you, you can watch your storyteller being developed. Allow your heart to open to how scary life was at times and how alone you often felt. ⌇

YOUR MIND-MADE ME

Because our parents left the meadow for the world of their minds, most of us as young children didn't have people who truly listened and helped us with all the overwhelming thoughts and feelings we were experiencing. So you, like most children, began to tell yourself stories about what was going on in order to try to manage your fear. And thus, the storyteller inside of your head, or what Eckhart Tolle calls "the mind-made me," was created. The wispy clouds that formerly passed through the meadow of your well-being begin to circle around your head, cutting you off from your heart and ensnaring you in the world of your mind.

"Mind-made me" is a very powerful way to describe what most people experience as themselves. The "me" you think you are is just a collection of thoughts, feelings, and beliefs based on fear. Your mind-made me is the storyteller that tries to manage Life, so hopefully you won't get lost in the fear, loneliness, and despair inside of you that you are so afraid of. I also like the term *mind-made me* because it alludes to the possibility of another sense of you. Not another "me," so to speak, but another place to live from—the meadow.

The creation of this storyteller in your head didn't happen overnight. Slowly, almost like putting together a ten-thousand-piece picture puzzle, you organized your experiences into a self-image that allowed you to feel the illusion of having some control over this huge thing called Life. The key here is the word *image*. It means "a likeness or representation of something." The storyteller is not Life—it has ideas about Life, and it generates clouds of struggle that cut you off from the living experience of Life.

Return to watching the movie screen and listening to the storyteller narrate the film. As you observe, you can see that at one moment the storyteller thinks of you as a good and "together" person. Then, in a flash, if somebody judges you or rejects you, that image can change into unworthiness, insecurity, anger, or self-judgment. That is how ephemeral your self-image is.

❦ Notice what is happening with your breath right now. Are you holding it because of what we are exploring? If so, imagine blowing out a candle for a few breaths before you continue reading. ❧

YOUR CHILD-MADE ME

At times I call the storyteller the "child-made me" because it is important to realize that the self-image you function from as an adult was created in your mind when you were a child. Psychologists say that the foundations of your view of yourself and of Life were well formed by the time you were six years old. So the beliefs, attitudes, wants, and fears that move through your head all day long—and that cut you off from fully experiencing Life—were created in the mind of a child.

❦ Take a moment and let in this truth: the clouds of struggle were formed in the mind of a child. If you are honest with yourself, you will see that most times you are pushed, pulled, prodded, and engulfed by thoughts and feelings that have been with you since you were very young: the longing to be liked, to be perfect, to be the best, to be safe, to be in control, to be right; the belief that you are less than or not enough; the sense that if only you were able to change yourself and your life, then everything would be okay. The stories that these beliefs spin in your mind may change over the years, but the essence of them is the same as when you were young. So if you look very closely at what goes through your mind all day long, you will see that the self-image you crawled into as a child is still alive and active inside of you. Breathe! ❧

If you could go back and be inside of yourself when you were two or three years old, you would be able to recognize the growing insecurity in your mind—the fear of your parents leaving, the devastation of being teased by an older child, the jealousy of having your sibling get the bigger Popsicle, the grief when a beloved toy was lost.

Next, if you were able to visit yourself when you first went to school, you would see how overwhelming it was. Growing up, we all had moments when we felt vulnerable and exposed. People said mean things to you, they used you, they judged you, they teased you, and they rejected you. Out of this arose the fears that you were not doing it right, were not good enough, or would be rejected. These fears followed you throughout your schooling, along with the deep fear that sometimes threatened to overwhelm you when you were alone: the fear that you wouldn't be able to keep everything together.

Then there was adolescence. The desire to fit in was one of the core things that ran you, and like most kids, you likely did some crazy things in order to belong. You may have starved yourself or scarred your face from squeezing your pimples. You may have put down other people in order to feel more powerful. The sad thing is that most children, even those in the "in" crowd, believe that they are not enough.

⸙ Go back to the theater again and push the button on your armrest that will rewind the movie to your adolescence. Allow a challenging experience from that time to show up on the screen. Can you allow this awkward, easily confused, and quickly embarrassed adolescent into your heart? ⸙

THE CONTINUATION OF CHILDHOOD FEAR

The fears of childhood don't go away. In fact, they get buried inside and then influence us from underneath our everyday awareness. Let's imagine, as you watch yourself up there on the movie screen, that you are attending a party, and let's listen to what might be going through your head: "I talk too much." "I don't talk enough." "Another drink will make me feel better." "She is prettier than I am." "I think I am doing this pretty well." "He could never be interested in me." "All I want to do is get out of here." "I don't know what to say." "I am better than she is." "What happens if there is a lull in the conversation?" "I am not smart enough to contribute to what she is saying." "I should have . . . I shouldn't have." "They don't like me." "I should be more outgoing." "I want another drink." "I was the life of the party." Even believing that you did the party right comes from fear that you could have done it wrong.

Then imagine what happens that night after the party, when you are awakened by the storyteller who critiques everything you said and did at the party, giving you a sinking sense that it wasn't okay. What doesn't show up on your screen is that the other people at the party are unconsciously run by these deep fears too, and they may very well be critiquing how *they* did. Fear is so embedded in us—and our fear of looking at it is so great—that one of the core functions of our storyteller is to keep us as far away from our fear as possible.

The fear-based storyteller doesn't only talk loudly about parties. There are all sorts of life experiences that bring its nagging commentary to the forefront of your mind. There may be an important business meeting the next day, a trip to a new destination, a visit with a challenging relative, or a doctor's visit about the lump in your breast. The storyteller's voice also shows up in the everydayness of Life: "I am going to be late." "I am not dressed right." "I followed the wrong directions." Whether it is everyday fears or the big ones, most people have some level of fear moving through their minds most of the time.

꙳ Settle into the theater again. Now push the button on your armrest that will take the movie to an embarrassing experience you had as an adult. Allow yourself to re-experience it as fully as you can up there on the screen. Recognize the voices of fear and self-judgment that arose inside of you. Know that these voices can be set free so that you can simply be yourself without fear or self-judgment talking away in your head. ꙳

THE PRICE OF FEAR

Most people are not aware of how afraid they are of Life. The story-teller inside of them believes that, rather than trust Life, it has to *do* Life and do it right, while secretly believing that whatever it does is not enough. Though your storyteller longs to be loved, it doesn't know how to love itself. It wants desperately to be understood by others, but it does not know how to be with itself in an understanding way. It is afraid of rejection and thus is usually concerned about what other people think of it. It often feels unworthy and becomes very busy try-ing to hide the so-called unacceptable parts of itself from the world. It feels a lot of guilt about the most inconsequential things (although it doesn't believe they are inconsequential). And this guilt fuels shame, the sense that there is something bad and wrong about itself.

Because of this chronic sense of struggle, the storyteller is con-stantly chasing happiness, believing that it will be happy when it does life right and thus gets everything together. But for everybody, this getting it all together comes and goes in a flash, and when it slips away, the storyteller is off again on the pursuit of happiness, trying to get what it wants and get rid of what it doesn't like. Can you feel how frustrating that is? Can you feel how heart numbing that is?

You pay a heavy price for living from your fear-based storyteller and then spending your life trying to outrun it. For this moment, can you notice the storyteller inside you that has been trying its whole life to keep everything together and the fear that generates this effort? Can you see that to be run by this struggling storyteller makes it impossible for you to experience Life simply and clearly?

As you were growing up, the more you were engulfed by the world of fear, the thicker your clouds of struggle became. In that world of fear, something even more debilitating happened: you became afraid of your own fear. So your life became a game of trying to feel good in order to leave fear behind. But the good feeling never lasted, because it was based on fear. And the more you got caught in the world of fear, the more you lost sight of the meadow of well-being within you.

When your endless trying doesn't bring the results you want (because you can never know the lasting happiness you long for within your clouds of struggle), you can then get even more lost in stories of shame, anger, or despair, which are also based in fear. Shame is the fear that you are not doing your life right. Anger is the fear that you are not getting what you want or that you are getting what you don't want. Despair is the fear that you never had or never will have what you want.

The shame, anger, and despair of your storyteller feed each other. Anger can go all the way from subtle irritation to white-hot anger at Life, at people who are not doing it right, and at yourself for doing the same. The storyteller then often gets caught in self-pity and feels like a victim, thus feeding despair, which can go from a little melancholy to full-blown depression. In this victimhood, the storyteller either blames others for its suffering—"If only he would . . ."or "Why did she . . . ?"—or it blames itself, which feeds the shame.

We have all experienced this vicious circle of shame, anger, and despair that can arise from the depths, taking over our lives. The despair that is at the core of this circle has some very dark, fear-based stories: "This is all there is." "It will never get better." "There is no way out of this darkness, and I am here because I have done it wrong." Most people are so afraid of this despair that rather than meeting it within themselves and thus freeing it up, they spend their lives trying to run away from it.

But remember, as you are watching the movie screen and listening to the conversations inside of your head, you have never left the meadow of your well-being. You mostly don't notice it because you have been so trained to listen only to your storyteller and to buy into the clouds of struggle. In order to unhook from the storyteller's stories, it is important to look deeply and clearly into its world.

❦ Lift your attention from the book and notice something outside of the voice of your storyteller, like the dance of shadow and light in the area around you or the sounds of Life as they appear and disappear. Know that the amazing unfolding of Life is always happening right outside of the world of your storyteller. ❧

OUR SHARED EXPERIENCE

Isn't it amazing that all of this is happening inside of you, underneath your everyday awareness? And not to just you. Most people have these ongoing conversations inside because they are identified with their own fear-based storytellers. I know it may not seem that way because most people are very good at putting on a mask and hiding their fear from themselves and from others. It is no accident that the root word for *personality* is *persona,* which means "mask." So don't be fooled by appearances, for they can be deceiving.

A friend once told me about a co-worker she truly admired—and envied—because this woman had a fancy car, designer clothes, and a high-powered job, which we think of as the trappings of success. One morning this seemingly together person asked my friend to come into her office, where she revealed she had tried to kill herself the night before because her life had no meaning. So know you are not alone in having a storyteller that is based on fear and glued together with judgment.

❈ Back in the movie theater, push the button that projects onto the screen somebody you think has it all together, like a motivational speaker or a famous doctor. You can hear the voices in their heads, just as you can in your own. As you begin to hear their inner voices, you recognize that these other people carry many of the same fears and judgments that you do. They may not fall into them as much as you do, but they have a storyteller too. ❈

The reason we may not be fully aware of all this fear happening inside of us is that we have been conditioned to run away from it as fast as we can. This conditioning is why we are such a compulsive society. We are so deeply afraid of our fear, our anger, and the despair they generate that we create elaborate systems for not seeing them. In order to avoid uncomfortable experiences, we turn to food, drugs, alcohol, busyness, to-do lists, the Internet, television, shopping, and other distractions to keep ourselves numb. We even use meditation to achieve a state we want and to get rid of the states we don't. We distract ourselves with astonishing fervor. Even though distraction may bring us temporary relief, it does not heal this underlying movement of fear.

GETTING TO KNOW FEAR

◄ Take a moment to dip the finger of your attention into the river of your experience. See it. Hear it. Fully experience it. This moment is different from any other moment of your life. In this moment of purely noticing Life, there is no fear. ▶

With the above pause, you lifted your attention out of the fear-based mind and used it to notice Life. The storyteller might have resisted doing this altogether, or after a moment or two of pure connection, it might have pulled your attention right back into the world of time, for fear needs time to exist. It needs stories of past and future in order to get a foothold in your mind. Every moment you let go of relating to Life through fear and instead open to Life truly makes a difference—even if it happens for just one second.

What counts even more is being able to see the fear that clouds your direct experience of Life. In order to see fear more clearly, it is helpful to recognize that fear affects your body as well as your mind. Watch yourself the next time you are suddenly startled or somebody judges you, and you will see your body tightening. Fear shows up in your body as a tension headache, trouble with your jaw, frozen shoulders, difficulty breathing, a stiff neck, stomach problems, a backache, and other physical problems. Many of your physical difficulties and illnesses are fueled by the contraction of fear, which constricts the healthy flow and functioning of your body. You are also conditioned to try to get away from your fear by numbing yourself through compulsions, and most of them also wreak havoc in your body.

When you live in fear-based stories, you *react to* Life. When you live from the meadow of your well-being, you *respond to* Life. In the meadow you relax; you are open and available to Life. When you are identified with stories of fear, however, you become tight; you resist, react, and manipulate. Take a moment and be honest with yourself about how much you live in reaction. Many times you react to little things your friends and loved ones say and create drama in your world—drama that is all based on fear. Remember that commercial where the wife asks the husband whether her jeans make her look fat? She fears he will say she looks fat, and he fears not saying the right thing. That is how so many people live their relationships. Fear prevents an authentic and truly intimate relationship with yourself and with others.

Fear causes you to contract rather than open, to protect rather than connect, to resist rather than respond, to survive rather than thrive. Fear constantly makes demands, and you have spent your life trying to meet them. You don't have to live your life with fear in charge. It is possible to come out of the trance of fear and live from the aliveness, openness, and joy of the meadow. Can you feel the relief of that truth?

❀ Take a moment and dip the finger of your attention into the river of sensations that is your body. Are you holding tension in one shoulder (or maybe both)? Are the muscles right above your pubic bone being tightly held? Is your brow furrowed or possibly your jaw clenched? Whatever tension you notice, for this moment, invite it to let go. ❀

THE WAY OUT

Whatever your storyteller does to attempt to get rid of fear only causes more fear. So the way out of fear is to get to know it through your heart. It is possible to become honest enough with yourself to be able to start looking at what goes on inside of you, and in that looking you become free. As soon as you become aware of the stories of fear you crawled into, you can begin to see through them and return to the meadow of well-being within you. The renowned writer and speaker Krishnamurti said in a talk in Paris in 1969 (published in the 1973 book *The Flight of the Eagle*):

> It is not that you must be free from fear. The moment you try to free yourself from fear, you create resistance against fear.

> Resistance in any form does not end fear. . . . [One] must understand the whole nature and structure of fear . . . that means learn about it, watch it, come directly into contact with it. We are to learn about fear, not how to escape from it, not how to resist it . . .

In order not to be controlled by fear and to do what Krishnamurti suggests—to look at your fear—it is important to ask, "Do I want to be free from fear?" Initially you might answer, "Yes, I do." That will probably be followed by, "But it is scary to look at my fears." That response is just fear, afraid of looking at itself. But when you really look at your fear, you will see that it is made up of stories that were conditioned into you when you were young, and they are nothing to be afraid of. I assure you, looking at fear is one of the safest things you will ever do, once you learn how to see fear rather than believing your fear-based stories.

I once heard a teacher talk about a dream she had many times. In the dream, a monster was chasing her, and she always woke up in terror at the place where the monster was about to get her. When she told a friend about the dream, her friend suggested that she turn around and look at the monster. That thought so frightened her that in subsequent dreams she kept on running. Then one night, as she was again running away from the monster, a wall appeared in front of her, blocking her escape. With great trepidation, she turned to look at the monster, and to her surprise, the monster stopped and didn't come any closer. She then noticed that the monster had pink fingernails. In that moment, she woke up and never had that dream again.

This dream represents the power of turning and looking at fear itself rather than letting it influence you from underneath your everyday awareness. At first, looking at fear is scary. But slowly you realize how scared your storyteller is, and you begin to see that it has been that way for a very long time. The fact that the monster didn't come any closer when the teacher turned and looked at it tells us something important: we are afraid that if we turn and look at our fears, we will be devoured by them, but this is not true. And the monster's pink fingernails signify how our fears actually are not as scary as we think they are when we are running from them.

I was raised in an environment that fostered terror, and I became so caught in the world of fear that in my early twenties I tried to kill myself three times because the intensity of the fear that I lived in was unbearable. My fear showed up as dread—the combination of feeling something really bad was going to happen and the belief that it would happen because I had done something very wrong. I tried psychiatrists, psychologists, group therapy, counselors, medications, affirmations, hospitals, meditation, hypnotherapy, and anything else I could find in order to try to outrun my fears.

It was only when I was taught how to turn toward my fear, becoming compassionately curious about these fear-based stories rather than trying to fix or get rid of them, that the pressure began to be released. Fear will always be a part of me, but whereas it used to be 100 percent of me, now it is only 5 percent. When it does arise, I can listen to it rather than getting lost in my fear-based stories. In that listening, fear calms down through the healing energy of my heart.

❮ What would it be like to get to know your fears rather than being afraid of them? Live in that question, rather than thinking you have to do anything about it. ❯

FEAR AND THE HEART

The novel *Magic Hour* by Kristin Hannah reminds me how deeply our fears long to be touched by the acceptance of our hearts. It is the story of a little girl who, at age four, is kidnapped and bound in a cave in the forest for a couple of years. She eventually gets free after her captor doesn't come back for a long time, and she shows up in a small town close to the forest. She lived without loving human contact for so long that she is like a wild child. She doesn't speak, she runs on all fours, and she howls.

A very aware child psychiatrist begins to work with her. What happens between the adult and the little one in the story speaks directly to the healing power of meeting fear right where it is. When I finished reading the book, I did something I have never done before with a novel: I immediately read it again, for it touched me deeply to watch this fictional girl come back to Life.

To me, the little girl is an extreme representation of the scared child inside all of us, and the psychiatrist is our aware, loving heart. She gives the girl what she most needs: loving presence. Rather than trying to fix or judge her, she meets her right where she is, and in that accepting attention, the little girl starts to slowly open to people. We can see how the strength of fear inside of her wars with the longing to trust the loving presence of the psychiatrist. As the little girl comes out of her shell, we get to hear how fear operates inside of her and how it is fueled through shame. We also get to see that it is the heart that heals.

You are the loving presence that your fears have been waiting for your whole life. It is your heart that will heal them. For the rest of this book, we will explore how your fear can heal through the accepting attention of your heart. Learning how to look, listen, and touch with kindness the stories of fear that have been driving you your whole life will free you from their grip.

❦ Are you breathing shallowly? Allow a deep, slow out-breath and recognize for a moment that your fear is afraid and needs the acceptance of your heart in order to let go. ❧

NO NEED TO BE AFRAID OF FEAR

As you come close to your deep fears, in order to give them the attention they need to let go, you will have moments when you will feel the fear of taking one more step closer to your fear. But remember, fear is nothing to be afraid of. It is just a story in your head, and 99 percent of your fears have never come true. A popular quote attributed to American writer Mark Twain says, "I have been through some terrible things in my life, some of which actually happened."

It is helpful to remember that fear closes you down, keeping you caught in the game of resisting Life, which builds a wall between you and Life. This wall of resistance stops Life from flowing through you, cutting you off from the joy of being fully alive. Would you rather keep fear locked up inside of you, generating everything from unsettledness to full-blown terror? Or would you rather rediscover the meadow of well-being by getting to know the fear-based storyteller in your head?

You don't need to be afraid of looking at fear. In order to discover the courage to look at your fears, it is important to know that even when you are caught in fear, it is happening within a greater space in you that is not afraid. This meadow of well-being has *always* been with you—it is within you even right now as you are reading this book—and it is absolutely okay with whatever is happening.

It is also important to know that our fear doesn't want us to be afraid of it. Instead, it wants to be seen, to be welcomed, to be touched by our hearts so it doesn't have to be afraid anymore. Or as poet and novelist Rainer Maria Rilke says in *Letters to a Young Poet*, "Perhaps everything that frightens us is, in its deepest essence, something helpless that wants our love."

You can discover how to bring accepting attention to fear. In fact, your fears have been waiting for you to be present with them your whole life. As you give fear the space to be, it then can pass through you, opening you again to the meadow of well-being within you.

❦ Check in with your body again and see if the place that you invited to let go a few pages back is holding again. Understand that it is fear that causes your body to contract. Open to one deep breath and invite this area to let go. Even if it tightens again, this moment of letting go matters. ❧

KEY POINTS

- Most people are caught in a low-grade fear that at times can flare into anxiousness, uncertainty, and even full-blown terror.

- Whether fear shows up as the slow drip of insecurity or comes to visit you in the middle of the night and shakes you to your core, it is usually fueling your storyteller's interpretation of your experience.

- The fears of our childhood don't go away. They get buried inside and then influence us from underneath our everyday awareness.

- We are so afraid of our fear and the shame, anger, and despair that it generates that we create systems for not seeing it, including compulsions, busyness, and endlessly trying to fix it.

- You pay a heavy price for crawling into the clouds of fear and then spending your life trying to outrun them. You don't have to live your life with fear in charge.

- Trying to get rid of fear only causes more fear. The way out is to get to know fear.

- Do you want to keep on running away from fear your whole life?

- The more you look and listen, the more your heart opens to how scared your storyteller is.

- You are the loving presence that your fears have been waiting for. It is your heart that will heal them and the other stories that your storyteller generates.

- As you allow fear the space to be, it can then pass through you, opening you again to the meadow of well-being.

- Don't be afraid of looking at your fears. Fear is always happening within a greater space in you that is not afraid.

•

•

•

REMEMBERING   Week 3
This week's Remembering Statement:
Fear is nothing to be afraid of.
Your own statement:

Remembering Session

We have explored that fear comes from your storyteller and that you have been deeply conditioned to fear Life. But we also recognized that fear is always happening within the greater space of the meadow of well-being. To turn on the calming aspect of your nervous system so that the clouds of fear can thin, we will add another pair of words to the "In . . . out. Deep . . . slow." you have been saying to yourself as you ride the waves of your breath.

The words are *calm* and *ease.* They are a part of a meditation that Thich Nhat Hanh, the beloved Buddhist monk and author, taught the children of his community. They are so powerful in soothing and focusing the mind that when the adults heard about them, they started using them too.

Think or say the word *calm* on the in-breath and *ease* on the out-breath. Allow yourself to feel these words rather than thinking about them. You are not trying to calm yourself. You are simply inviting calm and ease through feeling the essence of these words. If you have written the first two pairs of words on a card, add these now. Also, if these words resonate with you, you can use them any time to focus and calm your mind.

If you are timing your session, add one minute to the previous week's session, making it seven minutes. If time is not an issue, stay with each step as long as your curiosity is engaged.

Let's begin:

    ⸖ Close your eyes and dip the finger of your attention into the river of your experience, noticing what it is like to be you right now.

    For at least three in-breaths, tighten your muscles, and then very slowly relax everything on your out-breath as you say the great sound of letting go, *Ahh!*

    Bring your attention to your breath and relax into its nourishing circle, feeling the opening of the in-breath and the letting go of the out-breath. Remind yourself that for these few minutes you are inviting your mind to rest on your breath by saying silently to yourself, "In . . . out. Deep . . . slow. Calm . . . ease."

    When your attention goes back to the thoughts in your head, do not judge how often this happens but be willing to bring your attention back to the circle of your breath and the calming, focusing words.

    For a few moments at the end, open your attention to include your whole body. Notice what is different now that you have given yourself the healing of your own attention.

    When you are ready, open your eyes. ⸖

Abbreviated Version

❦ Close your eyes and dip the finger of your attention into the river of your experience, noticing what it is like to be you right now.

For at least three in-breaths, tighten your muscles, and then very slowly relax everything on your out-breath as you say the great sound of letting go, *Ahh!*

Bring your attention to the circle of breath and say to yourself, "In . . . out. Deep . . . slow. Calm . . . ease." When you notice that you are no longer paying attention to your breath, simply bring your attention back with no judgment.

At the end, expand your awareness and notice what is different after the conscious breathing.

When you are ready, open your eyes. ❧

4

You Are Not Alone

We have seen that the foundation of the storyteller is fear, and we've come to know the world of fear a little better. Now it is time to learn the art of turning toward your experience rather than being lost in it.

The first and most important step is to recognize you are not alone. There is an Intelligence that is with you every step of the way. If *Intelligence* isn't the right word for you, you may resonate with Presence, or Guides, or God, or the Beloved, or the Wisdom Self, or Angels. All allude to the same truth: that you are not walking the path of your life alone—you just think you are. So even though you may not recognize it, there is support that has always been with you and always will be. *Recognize* is the appropriate word, as what we are exploring here is a reknowing of this most basic truth of Life.

Oprah Winfrey, in her farewell show in 2011, spoke directly to this truth:

> I have felt the presence of God my whole life. Even when I didn't have a name for it, I could feel the voice bigger than myself speaking to me, and all of us have that same voice. Be still and know it. . . . It's always there speaking to you and wait- ing for you to hear it. In every move, in every decision, I wait and I listen. I'm still—I wait and listen for the guidance that's

greater than my meager mind. . . . So what I know is, God is love and God is life, and your life is always speaking to you.

Oprah used the word *God*, but I like what Stephen Levine said in a workshop I attended: "I can use the word *God* because I don't have a clue about what that means, but there is nowhere I see it not."

Most of us feel alone, with no sense of support, as we make our way down the paths of our lives. But even though we may feel alone, we aren't. There truly is something bigger than us that is speaking to us all of the time.

Imagine two fish jumping out of the water at the same time, and one says to the other, "Now I know what they mean by water!" The fish were so immersed in water their whole lives that they didn't recognize it. That's what it's like to discover this truth; we are so immersed in our clouds that they obscure the loving support that has always been with us.

THE SPELLS THAT KEEP US SEPARATE

The clouds of struggle that fill your head keep you cut off from the meadow of your well-being and the truth that you are not alone. These clouds include not only ideas about Life and stories of struggle, but also fear-based beliefs that you took on when you were very young. These beliefs are so deeply embedded in most of us that we are usually unaware of them. I like to call these core beliefs *spells* because they are perceptions that were superimposed on you; they are not true, and they can be lifted.

Rather than buying into the spells, you can learn how to see them and recognize how they generate habitual patterns of thinking that keep you lost in the clouds of struggle. There are eight core spells we all take on, and if you watch carefully, you will see they are all coming from fear. They can be divided into three types. The first two are what I call *foundational spells*. Then come the three *operational spells* that describe how we function after having taken on the first two foundational spells. Finally, there are the three *hidden spells*, which describe the core wounds we all carry from having identified with the spells.

Here is a list of the eight spells, broken down into the three types:

Foundational
- "I am separate from Life."
- "Life is not safe."

Operational
- "I must control Life."
- "I must do it right."
- "I am not doing it right enough."

Hidden
- "Because I am not doing it right, I am wrong."
- "I am unlovable."
- "I am all alone." (the core spell)

The Two Foundational Spells

Somewhere in the first year of your life, as thoughts began to drift through your head, you took on the first foundational spell: "I am separate from Life." You began to think there is a "me" inside of you who exists separate from Life, which is "out there." That is like one cell in your heart saying, "I am separate from the heart, and my life has nothing to do with all of the other cells that make up the heart, let alone the rest of the body!"

This spell of separation is truly insane, and it is the opposite of what is true. To help people on my retreats identify this spell, I often ask them to pick up a strawberry. I begin by telling them they are not holding a strawberry. They are holding the whole universe, because it took everything throughout all time and space in order for this strawberry to exist. We now know that every atom that makes up a strawberry was once part of a star, for stars were the incubators for most of the elements of Life. So this strawberry needed stars to exist. It also needed the creation of Earth and all of the creativity that has happened on the planet for the past 4.54 billion years. This brought forth the mother plant of this strawberry, which came from a seed, which came from another seed, and so on down through the corridors of time. Where does that continuum end? It is a thread of Life that goes all the way back to the beginning of our universe.

❦ Look up from reading this book and recognize that everything you see is made out of atoms that were once a part of a star. ❧

The strawberry would not exist without the sun that gives of itself day after day. It also needed water, a very rare substance in the parts of our galaxy that we have been able to explore. How could that water continue to circulate and give birth to Life without the atmosphere and all of the dynamics that make up what we call "weather"? This strawberry also needed mountains and trees that dissolved into soil, along with the bacteria and the worms in the soil that made it alive. It even needed the blue-green algae that oxygenated our planet billions of years ago and made cellular life possible.

So this one little strawberry needed all of the planet's creativity in order to live. It is dependent on almost everything for its existence. The same is true for you. It is purely an illusion that you are a separate being. Just as that cell in your heart is not separate from the other heart cells, your heart is not separate from the whole of your body, and you are not separate from the whole of Life.

You are intimately and intricately connected with absolutely everything throughout all time and space. Would you exist without the sun, stars, water, earth, and sky? No! Would your life be able to continue without bees to pollinate your food, workers who harvest it, people who drive the trucks to the market, or the people who drill for the oil that allows the trucks to run? We could go on forever. You are depen-
d___ ng for your existence, and thus you are connected

attributed to Albert Einstein says, "Many times a
much my own outer and inner life is built upon the
men, both living and dead, and how earnestly I
order to give in return as much as I have received."

The speaker of this quote was talking about the people who made his life possible. We are talking about *all* of the creativity of Life that is necessary for you to exist.

It is not only on the physical level that separation is an illusion. The interconnectedness of everything happens on all levels of existence. Take a look around the space you are sitting in and notice that it really seems that Life is just a collection of separate objects, including you. But science is now revealing to us that everything you can see is an outer expression of a field of energy, and this field connects it all at a very deep level.

It may help to imagine that Life is like a tree. This tree has roots you cannot see, and it is because of these roots that the trunk, the branches, the leaves, the flowers, and the fruit can grow. In the same way, everything you see arises from the root of Life, which is a field of energy, and in that field everything is connected everywhere at all times. This means that every atom, molecule, rock, bug, planet, bacterium, star, blade of grass, and person—including you—is a unique expression of this underlying energetic field. Not only are you unique, you are also a necessary expression of the same unified field. Just like a cell in your heart is a necessary part of a greater whole called your heart, you are a necessary and unique expression of the greater whole called Life.

What we are exploring here contradicts the concepts of Newtonian physics that we were raised with, the kind of physics that says that everything is separate. We're finally waking up from that dream. Physics is now helping us see what the great mystics have known forever: Life is like a spider web, and one tiny movement on the web is felt by the whole web. Lift your hand and wave it in the air. On some very deep level, the plants, people, and animals around you felt your movement. You are a part of this web, and your movements move the web.

So everything—absolutely everything—arises out of this web of being, is intimately connected to it, is animated by it, and then will eventually dissolve back into the web or field just like a wave in the ocean arises and then recedes back into the ocean. The wave is not separate from the ocean; it is the ocean temporarily expressing itself as a wave. The same is true for the people and things in your life. So in a very real sense, there is only one of us here! We are all just an outer expression of an interconnected web of being in which everything is dependent upon everything else for its existence.

    ❴ Lift your eyes from the book and take a moment
    to recognize that everything around you is just the
    expression of an underlying world of energy. ❵

It is hard for us to imagine that nothing is separate, that everything is interconnected. So take a moment to realize that we have bought into some pretty big illusions in the past. Think of the belief that the world was flat. People once laughed at scientists who said the earth was round. They said the idea was ridiculous and could easily be proven false because if the earth were round, everybody would fall off its surface!

The spell that we are separate from Life is a big illusion that appears to be true, but isn't. As we have been exploring, it does help to begin to see that on the physical and energetic levels nothing is separate. But it also helps to recognize how much suffering is caused by buying into this spell. If we are unaware that we are one family, we can believe that we are different from one another. So most humans are caught in the adolescent belief that my skin color, my politics, my beliefs, my sexuality, my opinions, my gender, my religion are better than someone else's.

This spell creates boundaries that separate us, whether it is in our intimate relationships, our politics, or our religions. The belief in separation even goes so far as to create artificial things called national boundaries, which we then fight over. Feeling we are separate from the earth has also allowed us to plunder and pollute her everywhere. Ultimately this spell detaches you from the unfolding of Life, causing you to lose trust in Life and in yourself. This, in turn, cuts you off from the pure joy of being alive. Seeing how far from the truth this spell is would be very funny if it didn't generate so much suffering.

The second foundational spell, "Life is not safe," stems from the first foundational spell and is one of the deepest illusions human beings take on. This is the spell of fear that we explored in depth in the last chapter. Life is a highly intelligent, benevolent, unfolding force that includes violence and death. Life is for Life, and it knows what it is doing. Yes, there is pain in Life, but there is much more suffering when you aren't open to its flow. Life is not always likable, but it is always *for* you.

    ❋ Take a moment to dip the finger of your attention into the river of your experience. Be curious about what it is like to be you right now. Know this moment in your life is unique. When you are fully present with this moment, you have stepped outside of your spells. ❋

The Three Operational Spells

This belief that Life is something to be afraid of brings forth the first operational spell: "I must control Life." This spell is like one cell in your heart deciding it has to beat and regulate the heart. This spell is so strong in the human mind at this stage of evolution that most people don't have a clue that what is in charge of Life is the Intelligence that has been orchestrating the dance of Life for billions of years and that regulates their hormones and beats their hearts.

This spell of control, the belief that you must *do* Life rather than *be* Life, generates the second and third operational spells: "I must do it right" and "I am not doing it right enough." This is the vicious circle most people live in most of the time: they try to do Life and do it right, all the while secretly believing they are not doing it right enough. This circles them back to the belief that they must do a better job of controlling themselves and Life.

True healing never happens through the struggle inherent in these three spells; it happens when you can see them and unhook from their stories. The peace and joy you long for don't come from changing anything; they come from the ability to see and unhook from your spells.

At first, the idea that you don't need to spend your time manipulating your experience of Life is a foreign concept. It is foreign because you (and most people) have been conditioned to believe that your job is to make your life be what you think it should be. In other words, you've been trained to try to create a particular reality rather than showing up for Reality.

As it dawns on you that trying to control Life only cuts you off from fully experiencing Life and that Life knows what it is doing, you begin to recognize the truth that it is safe to open to Life's creative, intelligent flow. Yes, that flow includes pain, loss, and death. We have tried to control Life in order to get away from these seemingly unlikable experiences. But the suffering we create for ourselves by resisting Life's flow is far greater than the pain we experience by being open to all of it.

Opening to the flow of Life can be very scary at the beginning, because the illusion of control gives you a false sense of protection, like walking the path of Life enclosed in a suit of armor. As you relax into Life, pieces of armor start falling away, and you feel unprotected and naked. To access the courage you need to let go of the illusion of control, ask yourself what would feel more alive: clanking through Life in heavy armor or freely walking, skipping, and dancing down the path?

It is courageous to contemplate the possibility that Life wouldn't fall apart or explode in your face if you didn't spend your energy trying to control it. But the more you awaken, the less interested you are in controlling Life and the more interested you are in connecting with it and opening to its creative flow, which includes both the dark and the light of Life. In that opening, you discover that the safest and the most creative thing you can do is to loosen your grip on control.

> ❧ Let go of reading and bring your attention to the circle of your breath. As it settles there, say silently to yourself, "In . . . out. Deep . . . slow. Calm . . . ease." Give yourself this gift for a few minutes. When you are ready, resume reading. ❧

The Three Hidden Spells
The longer you live from the operational spells, the more they strengthen the grip of the three hidden spells: "I am wrong because

I am not doing Life right," thus "I am unlovable," and that means "I am all alone." These are the secret fears that reside within all human beings and are so deeply embedded that most people are not even aware of them (most of the time), and when they are, they definitely don't want anybody to know they feel this way.

The "I am wrong" spell is the world of shame. Every human being experiences the type of self-judgment we call guilt, in which we decide we have done something wrong and guilt can be a useful tool for maneuvering through Life. Within most human beings, self-judgment has grown to enormous proportions, moving from the level of "I've *done something* wrong" to "I *am* wrong." Subtly, but sometimes quite loudly, this spell compares you to some mythical idea of who you should be and then berates you for coming up short of perfection.

Have you ever been afraid to tell a loved one the truth about a part of yourself because you were scared they wouldn't like you? That is the "I am wrong" spell that says, "I am not good enough, right enough, perfect enough to be loved." If you doubt you have this spell operating inside of you, imagine there is a machine that reads your thoughts and then announces them over a loud speaker—all of them! Like most people, you probably cringed when you imagined your secret thoughts being made public. If you closely examine what you don't want others to know about you, you will see the flawed logic at the core of the belief: "Because of these thoughts and actions, I am bad and wrong!" This spell can become so strong inside of you that it completely blocks your beauty, uniqueness, and perfection. It can freeze you out of Life.

The more you buy into the spell of "I am wrong," the more it draws you into the second hidden spell of "I am unlovable." This spell is so devastating because you need connection in order to survive. When you were very young, you were extremely vulnerable. Everything was much bigger than you were and definitely more powerful, and the primal need for survival was coded in your genes. Part of you knew that these giants you lived with (called parents) could either give or withhold the essentials: food, water, and shelter. Deep inside, you understood that pleasing your parents brought forth connection and not pleasing them meant pain. So you learned early on to be the "right" kind of child. Ram Dass, author of *Be Here Now*, calls it "somebody training"—learning the skills to be what you *should* be according to your family system and your society.

You put all this energy into becoming who you thought you had to be not only to get your needs met but also to earn the comfort of your family's attention, because attention is also necessary for survival. In the 1950s, Dr. Harry Harlow of the University of Wisconsin took a group of baby monkeys from their mothers at birth. The babies were put in cages and given a choice of two surrogate mothers. The first was a wire monkey that could feed them from a bottle suspended at its center. The second was a cloth monkey that, while it did not feed them, could be held close for comfort. Over and over, the baby monkeys chose the comforting cloth monkey over the wire monkey that could feed them. The nourishment of comfort was more important than the nourishment of food.

The more you feel lovable, the more connected you become with yourself and with Life. The more the "I am wrong" spell takes over—convincing you that you are unlovable—the more disconnected you become, and this makes you vulnerable to the last of the hidden spells: "I am all alone." This is the deepest fear inside of most human beings. In fact, when we lived in small tribes, the fear of banishment was more powerful that the fear of physical punishment.

The amazing thing is that the feeling of being alone is the opposite of what is actually happening. This is what we are exploring in this chapter. You have not been, nor ever will be, alone. There is support that is with you, guiding and loving you every step of the way. It is no accident that if you put a hyphen after the letter *l* in the word *alone*, you get *al(l)-one*.

❦ For a few precious moments, let go of everything except a full recognition that this is the only moment that matters in your life. The more your attention and your immediate experience come together, the more you will discover you are not alone. ❧

*

Not only are the eight core spells created out of fear and held together with judgment, but they also cause you to buy into the belief that you are all alone. You discover the untruths of these spells by using compassionate curiosity to see what you are actually experiencing. And the more you look, the more you can unhook from these deeply held beliefs you took on when you were very young.

To help you get to know the spells better, there is an appendix at the end of the book that lists the variety of ways that your storyteller may speak them. It can be very helpful to read this list and check off the ways that you recognize. Doing so will allow you to get to know your storyteller more intimately, which is the key to unhooking from it. Only then will you recognize the meadow of well-being that is the center of your being.

Being present with a particular spell opens the door into the contrasting experience. In my life, as I was able to be with my extreme self-judgment, that tightly held energy opened up into compassion. As I was able to be with my deep fear, giving it the accepting attention it needed in order to let go, my fear became a doorway into joy and a deep trust of Life. Or, as a friend once said, "Fear is just exuberance without a breath!" And, as I was able to be with my despair, I discovered that I am not alone.

❦ Pause for a moment and take a breath. Now exhale one long, slow out-breath and contemplate the possibility that you can discover how to see through your spells and live from the meadow of well-being within you. ❧

WHAT IS GOD?

In order to discover that you are not alone, it is important to explore the whole concept of God. Down through history, human beings have lived with some inkling that there is something bigger than us in charge, and in the Judeo-Christian culture, we have called it *God* (*Dieu, Dios, Dio, Gott, Elohim, Yahweh, Adonai*). Humans first saw this "something bigger" as supernatural beings that had to be placated by sacrifices and by doing everything "by the book." We then matured into the idea that God is a man with a beard who sits in heaven and decides whether we were good enough to enter. Gradually, instead of seeing God as a personification of a human being, more and more people began seeing God as an omnipotent being. Some believe God is a heavy taskmaster; others envision God as more benevolent. Either way, this all-powerful entity is still regarded as something "outside" of our individual selves.

We are now ready to take another step in our evolution of understanding God: that *God* is a verb. It is not a being or thing that can be defined, rather it is *Being* expressed in and through and as everything, including you. God is the unified field that permeates and animates all of Life. What is called *God* is the Intelligence at the heart of Life. This view takes God out of religion's ideology and rules and makes God available in the immediacy of our lives.

So how do you know that this Intelligence is with you, and always has been, as Oprah Winfrey declared? If you take just a moment to reflect, you will see that this is true. At one moment you were just one cell so tiny that it couldn't be seen with the naked eye, and it eventually multiplied into trillions of cells. As this multiplying happened, each of those cells knew which system they were to be a part of (like the circulatory system or the nervous system), and they knew exactly what their tasks were within that system. Now all of those trillions of cells digest your food, repair your cuts, beat your heart, and regulate your body's pH without a thought from you. In other words, you are a walking, talking sea of Intelligence.

❦ Pause for a moment, close your eyes, and open to the intricacies of this Intelligence at work in your body right now. Put your finger on your neck and feel the flow of blood pulsing throughout your body. Recognize the amazing creativity of all of your white blood cells that are protecting and healing. Now put your hand on your chest and acknowledge all of the work of each tiny alveolus in your lungs that allows oxygen into the bloodstream and absorbs carbon dioxide so it can be breathed out. All of this is the working of this vast Intelligence at the heart of Life. }⃰

The Intelligence that is running your physical body is just one facet of the vast Intelligence that is in charge of Life. It also permeates and penetrates all levels of your existence, including your mind and heart. The best word I have ever come across to describe it is *Presence*. Presence is always with you. You already have a relationship with it; you just may not notice it. It is always speaking to you, but you often don't hear it because the voice of your storyteller is so loud.

ASKING FOR HELP

There is a powerful story that Martha Beck, a long-time columnist for *O, The Oprah Magazine*, wrote in her book called *Expecting Adam*. It speaks directly to the truth that we are not alone and help is always here. This book is about Beck's pregnancy with her second child, Adam, who has Down syndrome. At the time she became pregnant, she had been at Harvard for many years, working on her undergraduate, graduate, and postgraduate degrees. Harvard revered the mind as providing answers to Life's questions, and so did Beck. But Adam changed all that. She says that before he was born, "I had to unlearn virtually everything Harvard taught me about what is precious and what is garbage."

As soon as Beck became pregnant with Adam, she started having experiences that could only be described as outside of the box of normal. In the fifth month of her pregnancy, while her husband was out of town, Beck was sleeping with her two-year-old daughter. When she woke in the middle of the night to a wet bed, she checked Katie's diaper only to find it dry. In the bathroom, she turned on the light and discovered herself covered in blood. (Later, she learned she'd experienced a placental abruption, which can be fatal to mother or child without medical intervention.)

Beck was so light-headed from blood loss that when she called the university's health services—there was no 911 in those days—and the nurse told her to come to the emergency room immediately, she was so weak that she was unable to tell them that her husband was gone and she didn't have a ride. After she hung up the phone, she started drifting in and out of consciousness, and as her normal perceptions faded, she felt presences in the room. She could not physically see or hear them, but she could feel them. "Their presence was as real and ordinary to me as the presence of oxygen," she writes in her book. She didn't know what these presences were. The normal terms, such as *angel, ghost,* or *spirit,* didn't work for her. She finally decided that the best word to describe the presences was *friend.*

As she grew weaker, she asked for help for her baby. She was very cold due to the loss of blood, but immediately after asking for help, she started to warm. And the bleeding stopped. Beck said the experience was extremely soothing. But then the presences left, and she became cold and dizzy again. She said she then did one of the hardest things she has ever done: she asked for help for herself. Immediately she felt a set of hands holding her, a wonderful warmth emanating from them. This calmed her deep fear, replacing it with a knowing that both she and her baby were out of danger.

"I did not 'fall' into sleep that night," Beck wrote. "I rose into it, out of the black, cold pool as though I were being lifted by a thousand wings." She was never quite sure what happened that night, but as her life force was fading, she accepted things she would have disbelieved at any normal moment.

What did make sense to her was that as she asked for help, she opened what she calls "a cosmic door" an inch or two. Beck could see that this kind of help had always been there for her—she just didn't know it. It also made sense that the reason she hadn't been aware that support was always available was that she didn't know she had to ask—and that asking opens a door.

THE POWER OF QUESTIONS

How do you ask for help? How do you discover that "friends" are always with you? First by understanding that you have been conditioned to believe in the two foundational spells: "I am separate from Life" and "Life is not safe." These brought you to the three operational spells: "I must control (do) Life," "I must do it right," and "I am not doing it right enough." And the three hidden spells of "I am wrong," "I am unlovable," and "I am all alone" tighten the noose of separation, cutting you off from help that is always there. Remember, when Beck asked for help for herself, she said it was the hardest thing she had ever done.

As long as you buy into the illusion that you are separate from Life and, because you fear it, you must be in control, you will be cut off from the vast Intelligence that is always with you. Be patient with this. You (and most everybody else) have been caught in these spells for most of your life. But you have now drawn into your life the shift of perception that will allow you to unhook from the spells and, in that unhooking, discover that you are not alone.

The most skillful way I have discovered to be in relationship with Presence is to ask questions without looking for an answer. This may seem strange at first because you are so used to asking questions and then trying to figure out the answer. But that approach asks your mind for the answers, and your mind is mostly lost in the clouds of your conditioning, cut off from the wisdom at the heart of Life.

Looking for answers in your mind often leads to tension and frustration. The mind works well for objective questions that have definitive answers, but have you ever closely watched yourself when you were trying to figure out the answer to a subjective question, such as "Should we get married or not?" or "Should I buy this car or not?" One moment getting married or buying that car seems like a good idea, and the next moment it doesn't. That is what it is like to use your mind for the answers to many of the questions in your life.

Instead, you can go directly to the Intelligence at the heart of Life. To ask a question and then let it go is one of the most powerful tools you can learn on this journey back to your being. The power of a question isn't in the answer; it is in the *question itself.* In some very deep and profound way, the answer isn't important. What is important is to simply ask a question, then bring your attention back to this immediate moment, allowing the question to work its magic from underneath your everyday awareness. Why is this so powerful? When you ask a question without looking for the answer, you are circumventing your mind and creating a space inside of you where the Intelligence of Life can be heard. It is guaranteed that Life will fill that space with the answer at the right time, for the energy of Life always fills a void.

You have experienced the truth of this many times in your life. A simple example is trying to remember another person's name. You go to your mind and you can feel the name is right on the tip of your tongue, but you are frustrated because you can't seem to get to it. You then go on with whatever you are doing, and a while later the name pops into your head. That is the mechanism we are talking about here. As soon as you let go of trying to find the name, the question you asked, "What is his name?" begins to work its magic, and up pops the name. The key is not to look for an answer. This can be challenging at first, for you are addicted to answers. Answers give you the illusion of control, but being in the space of a question allows you to live the answer, becoming a partner with Life.

❦ Dip the finger of your attention into the river of
sensations that is your body. Are any of your favorite
places of tension holding on? If so, choose one area
and tighten it on your in-breath and then, very slowly,
let it go on your out-breath. ❧

I was reading the novel *Maisie Dobbs* by Jacqueline Winspear, and there was a passage that poetically describes the themes we're discussing: "Truth walks toward us on the paths of our questions. . . . As soon as you think you have the answer, you have closed the path and may miss vital new information. Wait awhile in the stillness, and do not rush to conclusions, no matter how uncomfortable the unknowing."

Take a moment and let that in: "truth walks toward us on the paths of our questions." In other words, when you ask a question without looking for an answer, you create an opening where truth can speak to you. Asking such a question doesn't have to be uncomfortable. Many times it won't be. You just ask a question and let it go, knowing the answer will appear in the right time and the right way.

The power of asking questions without looking for an answer is like the power of a sacred talisman that is there for you no matter what is happening. You may not notice how powerful this is at first, so just keep on asking. In the beginning, the mind won't have a clue about the phenomenal power of asking questions. It will still look for an answer. It will also doubt that anything will happen, and it will forget to ask. That's just what minds do. But keep on asking. The fogginess of your mind that can't hear the answer will slowly lift, and you will live the answer.

Some of my favorite questions are:

- What am I ready to see here?
- What is the way through this?
- What do I need to say/do/be that is for the highest good?
- How can I serve?
- What am I?
- What is asking for my attention?

If these don't call to you, ask Life, "What are my questions?"

Most of us will experience the answers to our questions through a simple knowing, more like an *Aha*. You know what I mean—that moment when something clicks inside you and it's very clear that it's the truth. It may come to you in the shower, or it may be triggered by a sentence from a novel you're reading or a line from a movie. However it comes, the more you ask questions, the easier it becomes to *feel* the answers.

Also know that these answers won't necessarily arrive in your desired time frame. Asking a question signals to Life that you're ready to live the answer, and then Life lives it through you at the appropriate time. Because I have been asking questions for a long time, most answers easily and quickly appear within me. But there are questions I have lived in for years, and I am still growing into the answer. I know that the answers will come at the right time.

❦ Take a moment and ask Life to show you your spells. Then let that question go, so it can work its magic from underneath your everyday awareness. ❦

Through asking questions without looking for an answer, you have a conscious conversation with Being itself and discover you are not alone. Take the courageous step of knowing that Life is smarter than you and that it knows what it is doing. Turn the challenges of your life over to Life, over to that which is bigger than you and has been orchestrating the dance of Life for billions of years. Then be willing to listen, for Life is talking to you all of the time.

Finally, be willing to give yourself the gift of asking open-ended questions. The answers to your questions will be lived through you in Life's time and in Life's way. Your questions will help to undo the illusion of your spells, revealing to you the meadow of well-being that is always with you, the well-being that knows that no matter what is happening in your life, it is all okay.

KEY POINTS

- You are not walking the path of Life alone—you just think you are.

- The clouds of struggle that fill and surround your head include core beliefs you took on when you were very young. They can be called "spells" because they are concepts that were superimposed on you; they are not true, and they can be lifted.

- These spells keep you cut off from the support that it always with you.

- Believing that you are separate from Life has cut you off from a conscious conversation with the Intelligence of Life.

- Everything you can see is an outer expression of a unified field of energy in which everything is dependent upon everything else for its existence.

- Life knows what it is doing, and it is safe to open to its flow.

- Trying to control Life cuts you off from fully experiencing Life.

- *God* is a verb. God is not a being or thing that can be defined; rather, it is *Being* expressing in and through and as everything, including you.

- Presence is always with you; you just don't notice it. It is always speaking to you, but you don't hear it because of the noise of your storyteller.

- To ask a question and then let it go is one of the most powerful tools a person can learn, for the power of a question isn't in the answer—it is in the question itself.

- When you ask a question, the key is not to look for an answer. In the beginning, the mind will look for answers, doubt anything will happen, and forget to ask.

- Take the courageous step of trusting that Life is smarter than you and that it knows what it is doing.

- Turn the challenges of your life over to Life—over to that which is bigger than you and has been orchestrating the dance of Life for billions of years. Then be willing to listen, for Life is talking to you all the time.

-

-

-

REMEMBERING   Week 4
This week's Remembering Statement:
I am not alone.
Your own statement:

Remembering Session

In order to see more clearly all the spells that cut you off from the support that is always with you, it is helpful to discover what your storyteller is doing when your attention drifts back into the world of thought. For most of your life you have identified with your storyteller. In order to discover how to relate *to* it rather than *from* it, notice whether it is telling stories about the past or the future.

Read through these instructions, then put down the book and begin exploring. If timing your session, add one minute to last week's session for a total of eight minutes. If time is not an issue, stay with each step as long as your curiosity is engaged.

Let's begin:

❦ Close your eyes and dip the finger of your attention into the river of your experience, noticing what it is like to be you right now.

For at least three in-breaths, tighten your muscles, and then very slowly relax everything on your out-breath as you say the great sound of letting go, *Ahh!*

Bring your attention to the circle of your breath, saying the calming/focusing words, "In . . . out. Deep . . . slow. Calm . . . ease."

Ride the circle of your breath, and whenever you find yourself paying attention to your storyteller, notice if it is telling stories about the past or the future. If the stories are about the past, say "Past," then bring your attention back to the circle of your breath. If you notice the thoughts are about the future, say "Future," and then return to your breath. If you can't immediately see past or future, or if you are just spacing out, say, "Story." Then return to the circle of your breath.

For a few moments at the end, open your attention to include your whole body and notice what is different now that you have given yourself the healing of your own attention.

When you are ready, open your eyes. ⟩

Abbreviated Version

⟨ Close your eyes and dip the finger of your attention into the river of your experience, noticing what it is like to be you right now.

For at least three in-breaths, tighten your muscles, and then very slowly relax everything on your out-breath as you say the great sound of letting go, *Ahh!*

Bring your attention to the circle of your breath, saying the calming/focusing words.

When you find yourself paying attention to your thoughts, notice if the storyteller is telling stories about the past or the future, and name what you notice. If you are not sure, say "Story."

Bring your attention back to the circle of breath and the calming/focusing words.

Expand your awareness and notice what's different about your experience after a few minutes of being with yourself.

When you are ready, open your eyes. ⸕

5

The Healing Power of Curiosity

Before we move on to the next step of learning to see through your clouds of struggle, let's look at the work you've done so far. First, you are realizing how often you pay attention to the fear-based, judgmental storyteller in your head. You are also accepting that the foundation of these stories was created in your mind when you were a child, and that most of the stories are about how you want Life to be different than it really is. You have also begun to contemplate the possibility that you are not walking alone along the path of your life and that there is ever-present support available to you, especially if you ask for help.

Now you are ready to dispel your clouds of struggle so that you can recognize the meadow of this moment and rediscover how to relax into its flow. Remember, you have never left the meadow—you just think you have. And trying to fix, change, get rid of, or rise above your stories of struggle just leads to more struggle.

To reconnect with Life—to know again the joy of being fully alive—you need to see what is within you that blocks your full connection with Life. You need to get to know your clouds of struggle, including the spells (beliefs) they are made up of and the stories that are present when you are caught in a spell. This ability to see the spells that make up your clouds without identifying with their stories comes from the ability to look—to be with what you are actually experiencing with curiosity.

The best way I can describe this ability is through a metaphor I call the One Thousand Doors. Imagine being imprisoned in a room where every wall is filled with doors, and each one promises a way out. This room represents your struggling self. Some doors promise that if you fix your "problems," then everything will be okay. Others promise that if you just ignore them, understand them, deny them, try to numb yourself to them, or run away from them, you will be out of the prison.

You try 999 of the doors many times, and with each, one of three things happens: the door is locked, the door opens to a brick wall, or the door opens, and you walk through it, only to find yourself in the same room.

There is one door you have never tried. It is a very small door at the bottom of a dark corner. You can see there is a word written on its front, but you can't quite tell what it says. The first two letters are *he,* so you figure that is the doorway to hell, and you stay as far away from that door as you can.

But there comes a time after you have tried each of the 999 doors many times with no results, that you figure hell has to be better than this room. So you go over to the corner, crouch down in front of this little door, and much to your amazement, you see the word that is written on the front is *here.* You realize in a flash that this door is an invitation to be curious about your experience rather than always trying to make it be different than what it is. But this door looks too small to get through, and so your mind doubts that simple curiosity will help you out of this prison.

However, since everything else failed, you decide to give it a try. As you cultivate curiosity, an amazing thing begins to happen. The more you are curious, the more the door expands. Instead of walking through the door and out of the prison of your mind, you find the walls of the room slowly dissolving, until the room with a thousand doors is gone and you are fully connected to Life again.

THE ART OF LOOKING

❦ Stop reading for a few minutes and place your attention on the sounds around you. Notice that they are different than the previous times you have tuned into listening. Notice how they appear and disappear. Every single sound is brand new, even if you think you have heard it before. You are listening to the soundtrack of your life, and as you stay with it, you will hear that sounds arise and pass away. Be curious. There are loud sounds and soft sounds, sounds close to you and far away, even sounds inside of you. Stay with this listening as long as it interests you. When you are ready, come back to the book. ❧

In these few moments, you were curious about Life rather than thinking about it. Curiosity is the art of bringing your attention and your immediate experience together. As your attention becomes engaged with what is happening right now, you will discover that there is a whole lot going on around you that you never notice. It is Life, and when you are curious, you make direct contact with it.

We have all had moments when we were fully present for Life, but it is so easy to drift back into our stories about it. I hope you have now discovered that there is a big difference between your stories about Life and Life itself. It is also important to know that your storyteller is afraid of being this open to Life. It wants to pull your attention back into the clouds of stories in your mind. But with the power of curiosity, you can begin to see through your clouds and again be available to Life.

To discover the art of being curious, you first need to know that Life's pure energy is continuously pouring through you. As it flows through your mind and body, it gets condensed into ripples of thought, sensations, and feelings. But these are not who you truly are. You are awareness. You are that which can watch thoughts, feelings, and sensations pass through the vast spaciousness of who you really are.

To get a sense of this, close your eyes and silently say the word *peace* a number of times. If you watch carefully, you will observe that there is a part of you saying it and there is part of you that is aware that it is being said. This awareness is who you really are. It sees what is happening in any given moment and thus is not enmeshed in your thoughts, feelings, sensations, and experiences. Even if there are no thoughts in your head, you exist. Discovering this truth is the beginning of reconnecting with the meadow of your natural okayness.

You, like almost everybody else, have lost sight of the truth that you are that which can see and be with what is going on. Instead, you were taught to identify with your thoughts and the sensations and feelings they generate. You then were conditioned to fight what you are experiencing and to try to make it different than what it is. You learned how to resist what is showing up in your life, especially what is uncomfortable, through evaluating, judging, and trying to control your experience. But the truth is that denying, resisting, manipulating, and wanting your life to be different only causes more struggle and makes your clouds denser.

Ask yourself, "Has this approach of constantly trying to get to the good stuff and get rid of the bad stuff ever brought me lasting peace?" If you were honest with yourself, you would have to say no. Imagine watching a person who is busy trying to control the movement of the clouds in the sky. You can see how exhausting it is, and you can see that no matter how hard they try, it doesn't work. The person just becomes more frustrated and despairing. You can also see that they are so busy with the clouds that they don't notice the meadow or the rest of Life. The same is true for trying to control the clouds in your mind.

If you start looking at the stories that make up your clouds, you will see at their core an inner heaviness, which you listen to all day long. You may secretly fear that you are not good enough or you will fail. You may experience anxiety, shame, and unease. You may be afraid people will judge you, take advantage of you, or stop loving you. And you, like most people, want to be in control and are addicted to approval.

Yes, you have happy moments, kind moments, and delightful moments, but they quickly go away when something happens that your storyteller doesn't like, for you believe that your happiness depends on the events and circumstances of your life. Most of the time your storyteller struggles with everyday things, but when a major challenge comes along, it doesn't know how to respond and gather the gifts that are always inherent in challenges. That's because the storyteller is so used to reacting to Life. None of this is to be judged; it is just the way the ordinary human mind functions.

If, instead of judging, you really look, you will see that your greatest suffering comes from buying into the struggles in your mind. The only problems you have are in your mind. Yes, you have challenges, but the storyteller turns them into problems and then chews on them like a cow chews her cud. Your suffering also comes from resistance to experiencing what you are actually experiencing. All resistance does is thicken your clouds. The more you resist your experience, the tighter you get inside. The more you get caught in the clouds in your mind, the more you find yourself cut off from Life.

 ❦ Close your eyes and notice that you are sitting. You are not running, taking a shower, or standing in line at the post office. All of the millions of moments of your life have brought you to this moment, in which you are reading this book. Ask yourself, "How do I know that I am sitting?" Can you feel the place where your buttocks meet the chair? Is there pressure there? Is there maybe a tingle or a pain? Do not discount the power of just a moment or two of recognizing exactly what you are experiencing. ❧

Did you pause for a few moments and give yourself your own attention? Know that this is one of the most powerful things you can give to yourself. If you didn't do it, just notice how strong that urge is to be anywhere except here with yourself.

THE ADDICTION TO FIXING

One of the mind's favorite ways of staying distracted and far away from what you are experiencing is to create problems and then try to figure out how to fix them. In fact, it could be said that your mind is a problem factory, churning out problems all day long. It is astounding to recognize that once it solves one problem, there is usually only a very short period of time before it comes up with another problem. We are problem-fixer addicts.

How does this addiction affect your life? Imagine yourself back in the meadow. Then imagine yourself engulfed in clouds and holding a completely tangled ball of yarn, with your whole focus on trying to unravel it. You aren't available to the meadow. You don't even see it. Instead, you are lost in the clouds in your mind and lost in trying to fix the latest problem, which is represented by the ball of yarn.

Because of the problem factory, you are constantly trying to manipulate the world so it won't show up in ways that bring up the fear-based beliefs of your storyteller. You try to change your mate so he or she doesn't make you uncomfortable. You will stay in abusive relationships because you're afraid of experiencing the feeling of being alone. You will not get up from a meeting early, even if you have to go to the bathroom, because you can't face the fear of people judging you if you leave. Your problem factory may get you to spend lots of money on your hair, exercise programs, diet products, self-improvement classes, self-help books, and even meditation lessons—all in hopes that you will be accepted (and thus won't feel rejected). Then, when you've fixed one problem, your problem factory inevitably comes up with another. Yet trying to fix the problem factory is only more fixing.

It is important to understand that, even though you have been taught to believe that your mind is in charge of Life, it was not designed for this task. It is an exquisite tool for maneuvering through your life, but it is not supposed to be in charge of it. Life is in charge of your life, and it does a lot better job than your mind does. In fact, all of the violence, hatred, and aggression on our planet have been created by people who were lost in the clouds in their minds and reacting to their storyteller's fear and judgment.

Giving your mind the task of being in charge of your life is like giving a child the keys to a car. Children are so small that even if they could get the car to move, they couldn't see where they were going. Handing your mind the keys to your life will have you driving down the road of Life blind, because you truly can't see what is going on right now, much less what is going to happen next. Putting your mind in charge of your life has twisted it into knots of neuroses, and when you see this, you can see why we are such a depressed, disconnected, and addicted society.

The truth is, Life isn't under your control. Nor should it be. The mind is so changeable that at one moment it will tell you, "Yes, let's do that," and in the next it says, "No, don't!" For heaven's sake, you can't get your thoughts to be the way you want them to be for more than a few minutes, and yet you think that the constantly changing world of your mind is what should be in control of Life!

You can learn how to use your mind to be curious about Life rather than always attempting to control it, and you can learn how to stop arguing with Life. One of the greatest joys of awakening is to realize that you don't need to control Life. The joy and freedom that you long for come from connecting with it, and curiosity is the key to that connection.

> ⸓ Let go of reading the book and bring your attention to the circle of your breath, becoming very curious about what your breath is like right now. Do you feel it in your nose or in your chest? Does your belly move when you breathe? Do your arms move? Just be curious about Life expressing through you as your breath. What does your storyteller do as you are invited to notice your breath? ⸓

CURIOSITY: THE OPPOSITE OF FIXING

A deep and nourishing connection with Life comes when you can see through your addiction to trying to change yourself and change your life. As long as you are trying to change something, you are caught in the clouds of struggle, cut off from the meadow of your being and a direct experience of Life. True and lasting well-being doesn't come when you're lost in trying to fix a problem. Or as Einstein is reported to have said, "You cannot solve a problem from the same consciousness that created it. You must learn to see the world anew."

Curiosity is what enables you to tease your attention out of the problem factory of your mind so you can see your experience anew.

The more you become curious about what is going on right now rather than trying to make things be different than what they are, the more you will get to know your storyteller and the more you will be able to unhook from its stories. If your mind were an eight-cylinder car, then your addiction to fixing and changing your experience is like using only one cylinder, while using curiosity is like using all eight cylinders.

A clear way to describe the kind of curiosity we are talking about is focused attention. What do I mean by that? Focused attention is like a laser that, with its concentrated beam, brings the healing power of curiosity to your immediate experience. It allows you to see your storyteller more clearly in order to unhook from it and to come back to what is showing up in your life—not a story about your life, but the real thing. Focused attention results from being honest with yourself about what your mind, your body, and your emotions are doing in any given moment. It enables you to be present for what you are experiencing before you think about it.

With the honesty of curiosity, you can learn to watch the storyteller in your head without identifying with whatever story it's running at that moment. For example, when your storyteller is caught in a story of fear, you can move from saying, "I am afraid" to "This is a story of fear." You can also use curiosity to be with emotional pain. Without falling into the pain or suppressing it, you can describe it; perhaps to you it feels like "a ball of tears in my chest." You can even use curiosity to explore physical pain rather than trying to escape it.

What we are talking about here is the ability to relate *to* what you are experiencing rather than relate *from* it. This is why I love to use the word *curiosity* so much. The focused attention of curiosity enables you to rediscover your natural inquisitiveness. This kind of curiosity isn't about gaining knowledge. It is about accessing knowing by looking directly at what is happening right now. I like to call it "knowticing," putting together the two words *knowing* and *noticing*.

Once you become curious about Life, you begin to see that your focused attention transforms things. Your attention is like the sun: it can dispel even the deepest of emotional states bound up inside of you, just as the sun can dispel clouds in the sky.

The states that you are so afraid of—fear, despair, anger, and shame—are just trapped energy that you have been trying to get away from your whole life. They are like a bear in the woods. If you run away from the bear, it will run after you. If you stand and face the bear (unless you are between a mother and her cubs), the chances are the bear will leave. In a similar way, when you try to escape the inner states you deem uncomfortable and unacceptable, they pursue you, taking over your life and often leading to depression and anxiety. Turning toward them and giving them your full attention gives them the spaciousness they need to leave you. Every time you focus your attention on them—for a moment here and a moment there—you open yourself a little more to the flow of Life.

The mind is afraid of doing this at first. It is afraid that if it lets go of trying to control its experience and instead looks at it with curiosity, then either something bad will happen or nothing will happen at all. So the last thing the mind wants to do is to experience what you are experiencing. In fact, the mind will help you hide from experience, for the mind is a masterful denial and distraction machine. It will stay busy. It will daydream. It will distract itself with iPods, iPads, and TV. It is addicted to judging itself, lost in the endless game of trying to make itself better. It also loves to make other people responsible for its feelings, and it even indulges in compulsions that could kill it, all in order not to experience what you are experiencing.

Through the power of your own curiosity, you can see what your mind is doing. You also can discover that the safest thing you will ever do is turn toward your experience rather than turning away.

≪ Put down the book and connect with the circle of your breath for a few minutes. Whenever you notice you are paying attention to your storyteller again, be curious whether your stories are about the past or the future. ≫

When you stop trying to fix Life and instead become present for your own experience, you come into alignment with Life. This is where the clouds of struggle thin, for when you learn how to be fully present with the spells of fear that you have been operating under, it becomes easier and easier to unhook from them. The more you unhook, the more the wisdom and support of the meadow of your being become accessible. You then know again the joy and ease of showing up for Life, allowing it to unfold through you rather than always trying to control it.

NOTHING TO BE ASHAMED OF

Before you learn how to use your curiosity to transform your clouds of struggle, it is essential to understand that there is nothing inside of you to be ashamed of. First of all, the stories that pass through your mind all day long and that fuel your feelings are all stories you learned from your environment when you were very young.

Remember, at one time there were no thoughts in your head. When you showed up out of mystery as an infant, you had no ideas about Life—none at all. You experienced Life by feeling it, and the unconscious giants that were your parents were full of every feeling a person can have: anger, sadness, fear, love, confusion, judgment, kindness, jealousy, shame. Just as you learned language by listening to it, you learned the language of unconsciousness by feeling it.

When you were young, you were wide open to Life, and you could feel what was happening inside of the people around you. For example, if your parents were arguing down in the basement and you were up in the attic, you could still feel what they were experiencing, even though you couldn't hear them. You couldn't usually make sense of it, but you experienced it. What you were absorbing from the adults around you became the building blocks of your view of yourself and of Life, and this view was fully formed by the time you were six.

Did you have a choice of the verbal language you learned when you were young? No. If you lived in Japan, you learned Japanese. If you lived in France, you learned French. In the same way, if you lived in an unconscious family, as many of us did, you absorbed the language of unconsciousness that is based on fear, glued together with judgment, and has at its foundation the despair of feeling separate and alone.

Your view of Life was formed by what you absorbed from the inner world of the adults around you and also by what they said and did. At times they acted in ways that truly confused you. You noticed every-thing when you were young, including the times when what they said and what they were feeling were different. They would yell at you, but say they were not angry. They would tell you to be kind, but then talk about people behind their backs. They would say that they loved you, but often would either ignore or shame you when you were in need of connection.

There was so much happening around and inside of you as you were growing up, and mostly you were on your own to try to understand it all. You, like most children, probably had adults around you who couldn't help you be with what you were experiencing. So over time, more and more feelings were not able to pass through you. Instead they became frozen inside of you, cutting you off from the flow of Life. Out of this disconnection and confusion, you retreated into your mind, getting lost in your storyteller's attempts to always control what was going on.

Your stories were built out of the view of a child who was trying to make sense of the world and protect itself. But children don't have the perspective to discern what is truly going on, so they add two and two together and come up with twenty-two. For example, one of the most common stories at the core of your child-made me is that you were to blame for anything unpleasant in your family. Because children are the center of their own world, when uncomfortable and scary things happen, all they can assume is that they are the ones to blame. There was once a study of children who went through a divorce. Even if they were told they didn't cause the divorce, kids younger than age twelve secretly felt they had.

Another core story of your child-made me is based on the "Life is not safe" spell. Life was big and scary, and it seemed to bruise and abandon you over and over again. So you began trying to control this constantly changing river of Life in order not to feel the deep fear of being overwhelmed or abandoned. Over time, this urge to control became what we are calling the storyteller, the voice inside your head that is always talking, always trying to *do* Life and do it right so that it doesn't have to feel the deep fear and despair that are always under-neath its everyday awareness. The more you came to believe that the storyteller was who you are, the more disconnected you became from yourself and from Life.

It is important to know that you are not alone in being nutty as a fruitcake! We all took on the unconsciousness of our parents, just as they did from their parents, and so on and so forth all the way back through history. This also happened to your friends, your loved ones, your next-door neighbors—everyone. At this point in our evolution, everybody takes on the craziness of unconsciousness.

To get a sense of what I am talking about here, imagine that when you were born, you showed up in a huge warehouse that was filled with piles of Lego pieces sorted by shape, size, and color. Each pile represented an aspect of the human mind, like self-judgment, sadness, happiness, loneliness, rage, kindness, anxiety, exuberance, doubt, hope, or skepticism. Your job was to build a Lego spaceship (the storyteller in your head), and the only requirement was that you had to take at least one Lego from each pile. The result was that inside you (like inside everybody else) are all the variations of anger, fear, grief, and shame that make up our storytellers. Each person puts their Lego ship together differently, so you may have more sadness than anger, more grief than fear, or more kindness than meanness. But everything a human being is capable of is inside of you.

Most people crawl into their Lego spaceship, and it carries them through Life. What you are being invited to do is spacewalk. You are discovering how to step out of the storyteller's Lego spaceship and look at it, so you can unhook from its stories. One of the reasons I offer groups and retreats is so people can discover a place where they can be real and thus find out that everybody else has felt whatever they are feeling at some time in their life—and may even be feeling it right now.

So there is absolutely nothing to be ashamed of. Yes, you have made mistakes in your life, but mistakes are just "mis-takes" coming from the clouds in your mind, and they deserve to be forgiven. Remember, the foundational spells (beliefs) out of which your clouds operate were created inside you before you were six. Yes, your clouds have evolved over the years, but the origins are the same. If you are willing to look without judgment at the spells and stories that make up your clouds, they will fuel your awakening. Finally, you are not alone in how crazy your clouds are. Contrary to appearances, everybody else has a similar neurotic storyteller.

❦ Take a moment and ask yourself, "What is showing up right now?" Allow your experience to reveal itself like a Polaroid picture developing. Whatever you notice, say to yourself, "I am okay just as I am." See what your storyteller does with that statement. ❧

NOTHING TO BE AFRAID OF

The only power your storyteller's beliefs have over you comes from your unwillingness to look at them. At the beginning, none of us wants to look. It is like we are children hiding under our blankets because we thought we saw a monster in the closet.

When you first come out from underneath the blanket of your resistance, you may still have your hands over your eyes. When you discover the courage to peek through your fingers to look at what is going on inside you, you begin to see that maybe the parts you have been afraid of aren't monsters at all. As you drop your hands and really look, these parts appear no more substantial or monstrous than a pile of clothing thrown in your closet.

The deep feelings you have run away from your whole life are just like that, too. They are just the mirage of something you were conditioned to be afraid of. Having been raised in terror, and having had this terror affect my life for decades, I can tell you from experience that as I turned and met the terror, I discovered it truly was nothing to be afraid of.

You have been completely brainwashed into the belief that if you just don't look, the uncomfortable and unacceptable parts of yourself will go away. But, as you have discovered, they don't. All the feelings you stuffed are still there inside, influencing you from underneath your everyday awareness. You usually experience them as a low-grade sense of unease, but sometimes they come roaring up at the most inopportune times, engulfing you with their energy. Then that becomes more fuel for the belief that if you let the cat out of the bag—if you actually allow yourself to experience what you are experiencing—then you will be taken over by your feelings. But the opposite is true. Curiosity is your sacred talisman, for when you are curious about what you are experiencing, you are relating *to* it rather than *from* it. The more you do this, the less you will fall under the spells.

For a long time in your life it was important to stay in denial and keep these feelings at bay. You didn't have the skills that were needed for bringing your attention to your immediate experience rather than becoming lost in it. But as you learn the skill of being curious about what is going on inside, you can be with these feelings without becoming caught in them. That is what they need in order to be transformed back into the free-flowing aliveness that you are.

Yes, it takes courage to face and embrace what Life is giving you, especially when times are difficult, but this is how you come back to Life. To know the joy of directly experiencing Life, you have to be able to feel what you are feeling and bring it the light of your compassionate attention in order for it to move through you. This is a grand adventure of opening what has been closed inside of you so that your energy can flow freely again and you can know the joy of being alive. As you work with this book, the intent of your life will change from orchestrating your life (in order to feel good) to experiencing your life fully—including what feels good and what doesn't.

It is important to know this isn't just about feeling what you are feeling. When most people try to feel what they feel, they get lost in emotion because they identify with it. We tried that for years without much success in bringing forth lasting well-being. This was seen in the Primal (Scream) Therapy of the 1970s, which taught that if we just screamed out our anger, it would be released. It didn't work, and thus you don't hear much about Primal Therapy any more. What we are talking about is *meeting* what you are feeling. Yes, there are feelings there, but you are bearing witness to them rather than falling into their stories.

You also begin to realize that trying to feel good is like chasing the pot of gold at the end of the rainbow. At times you may think you capture it, but it always seems to slip away. However, when you are willing to let go of trying to make your life be a particular way and instead open to what Life is giving you without getting lost in stories, you begin to know joy. You may experience happiness for a while by getting what you think you want, but joy is the ability to be with whatever is happening.

❦ Is your storyteller liking or disliking what it is reading? ❧

YOUR BODY AS YOUR FRIEND

Applying the power of curiosity to your body can deepen your ability to experience what you are truly experiencing. Most of the time, you are not even in your body. You are caught in your mind and see the body as just a vehicle for carrying the mind around. But your body is one of the best friends you have on the journey back to Life. It is full of wisdom and will tell you exactly what you are experiencing long before your mind will. It is communicating its wisdom to you all the time, but you were not taught how to listen to it.

Let's take a moment to listen.

❦ Bring your attention to your body for just a minute or two and find three distinctly different sensations. Don't rush this. Just be curious and the sensations will reveal themselves. You could notice warmth, cold, tingles, throbbing, stabbing, aching, lightness, pressing, fullness, or hunger. Name for yourself what you are noticing. Again, your attention will drift back at times into your storyteller. There is no reason to judge this. Simply notice you've wandered into your mind again and bring your attention back to your body. When you are ready, resume reading. ❧

Did you pause and connect with your body? If you didn't, no judgment. You have spent most of your life far away from the wisdom and joy of your own body. However, do acknowledge your resistance. If you did turn your attention toward your body, your mind may very well have become bored because it is used to the manic activity of your storyteller. So you may have wandered off, thinking about the past or the future or, after a few seconds, just wanted to get on with reading the book. But know that every time you return your attention to the sensations of your body, you are clearing away a few more clouds in your mind and revealing more of the meadow of your being.

Feeling your way back into your body opens you into a field of joy and aliveness for which you are homesick. It is one of the most healing things a human being can do. Turning your attention to your body will also allow you to be more intimate with yourself, to discover that your body is speaking to you at all times and that its wisdom is amazing. This will help you see more clearly what stories you are running in your head instead of being at their mercy, for your spells express themselves as patterns of holding in your body.

*

What we have been exploring here is what I call "alchemy." We used to believe alchemy was about changing lead into gold. True alchemy is about transforming unconsciousness into consciousness. It is about discovering how to relate *to* what you are experiencing, rather than *from* it, by being curious about what is going on right now. Curiosity is where magic happens. My first teacher said, "In the seeing is the movement." He showed me that you don't need to fix, change, get rid of, or judge your stories. All you need to do is see them and see that they really are just spells you took on when you were very young that show up as the storyteller in your head, generating sensations and feelings.

The more you watch your experience with curiosity, the more you discover how to unhook from the foundational spells of "I am separate from Life" and "Life is not safe." This allows you to get to know the three operational spells: "I must control Life," "I must do it right," and "I am not doing it right enough." This brings you to the three hidden spells: "Because I am not doing it right, I am wrong," "I am unlovable," and "I am all alone."

The more you get to know your storyteller, the more these spells will simply pass through you, and the more easily you will see that only a small part of who you are is struggling with Life. The rest of you is at peace in the meadow of your being that is always with you right here, right now.

KEY POINTS

• To know again the joy of being fully alive, you need to get to know your clouds of struggle—the spells (beliefs) they are made up of and the stories the storyteller tells when caught in its spells.

• Denying, resisting, manipulating, or wanting your life to be different only deepens struggle.

• The mind resists Life by creating problems and then trying to fix them. Once it solves one problem, it comes up with another.

• You can learn how to use your mind to be curious about Life rather than trying to control it.

• The more you become curious about what is going on right now rather than always trying to change things, the more you will get to know your clouds and the more they will thin.

• There is nothing inside you to be ashamed of or afraid of.

• The only power your storyteller's spells have over you comes from your unwillingness to look at them. And, at least at the beginning, none of us wants to look.

- You have been conditioned to believe that if you don't look at the uncomfortable and unacceptable parts of yourself, they will go away. But they don't.

- Fully experiencing Life without the filter of our storyteller is what we all deeply long for.

- The mind is afraid of looking, so it will do all sorts of things to distract you from being curious.

- As you turn your attention toward yourself, you are not trying to make anything happen. All you are doing is being curious about your immediate experience.

- As you see your spells, you will see through them, bringing your attention back to the joy of being fully here for Life, right now.

-

-

-

REMEMBERING   Week 5
This week's Remembering Statement:
What is showing up right now?
Your own statement:

Remembering Session

Learning how to dip the finger of your attention into the river of your experience will change your life. You will be much less a victim of what is happening and more able to transform your experience through the power of focused attention. But if you're like most people, the muscle of your attention is probably flaccid. Your attention has been caught inside your mind for so long, being pulled from one thought to another all day long, that you have lost the ability to be simply curious about what is happening right now. In each of the Remembering Sessions, you have been flexing your muscle of attention so that it becomes strong enough that you can be curious about what is going on right now.

You started strengthening your attention by being curious about the circle of your breath. You were then connected to the power of deepening your breath through the candle breath and invoking peacefulness through the calming/focusing words. The next step was to discover how to watch your storyteller by noticing whether it is telling stories about the past or the future.

Now it is time to deepen your ability to be present for yourself through feeling your way into your body, exploring what you are experiencing in different areas. Doing so will bring your attention and your immediate experience together. As you explore, you will see how far away from your body you usually are. You will also see how, when your attention is fully engaged with what you are experiencing, any tension held in your body can begin to release.

Remember, you are not trying to make anything happen. You are not even trying to meditate. All you are doing is being curious about your immediate experience by bringing your attention to your body. This is what I mean by "knowticing": the art of using your attention to notice what is happening without trying to make anything happen. In this kind of noticing, knowing can arise.

Read through these instructions and then set down the book and begin exploring. If you are timing your session, add one minute to the previous session for a total of nine minutes. Trust yourself on the amount of time. If nine minutes is too much, shorten it a bit. If time is not an issue, stay with each step as long as your curiosity is engaged.

Let's begin:

❋ Close your eyes and dip the finger of your attention into the river of your experience, noticing what it is like to be you right now.

For at least three in-breaths, tighten your muscles, and then very slowly relax everything on your out-breath as you say the great sound of letting go, *Ahh!*

Bring your attention to the circle of your breath, saying the calming/focusing words, "In . . . out. Deep . . . slow. Calm . . . ease."

Now bring your attention to a place in your body that interests you. It could be a place where the energy is open, generating wonderful sensations, or it could be a place of holding. If no place is calling to you, bring your attention to a place where you chronically hold tension. Rather than turning away from it, turn toward it, being curious about what is happening in this area. There are many sensations happening there, and they are like creatures in the forest. If you sit quietly and are patient, they will reveal themselves to you.

Here are some questions to keep your curiosity activated:

- What am I experiencing here?
- How big is it?
- What is the nature of the sensations (aching, throbbing, tingling, for example)?
- Do the sensations have a definite boundary?
- Do the sensations move around or stay in one place?
- Do the sensations stay the same or change?
- Is what I'm feeling on the surface or deeper in my body?

As you allow your attention to settle on a single
area, many different sensations will reveal themselves.
Whenever you find your attention has wandered back
to your storyteller, bring it back to this area and be
fascinated by what you can discover.

Now gently breathe into this area. Touch this holding
from the inside with your own breath, allowing the touch
to be as soft as a mother's caress.

Stay with this exploration as long as it interests you.
It may be thirty seconds or a number of minutes.
Don't force it, but be willing to remember that huge
gifts come out of the ability to have your attention
present for what is happening in your body.

When you feel complete with your exploration, come back
to the circle of breath and the calming/focusing words.

For a few moments at the end, open your attention to
include your whole body and notice what is different
now that you have given yourself the healing of your
own attention.

When you are ready, open your eyes. ❧

Each day you can explore another part of your body with this kind of
depth. Remember, what you experience will develop like a Polaroid
picture under the light of your attention. As your attention settles
in an area, it may seem like not much is going on. But as you stay
there, the full variety of sensations happening in that area will make
themselves known to you. It is under the gaze of your compassionate attention that bound-up energy, if it is ready, can begin to move
and let go.

Abbreviated Version

❦ Close your eyes and dip the finger of your attention into the river of your experience, noticing what it is like to be you right now.

For at least three breaths, tighten your muscles, and then very slowly relax everything on your out-breath as you say the great sound of letting go, *Ahh!*

Bring your attention to the circle of your breath and the calming/focusing words.

Now bring your attention into your body by exploring an area with great curiosity, allowing the sensations to reveal themselves. Gently breathe into them.

When you feel complete with your exploration, come back to the circle of breath and the calming/focusing words.

At the end, expand your awareness and be curious about your experience after having given yourself the healing of your own attention.

When you are ready, open your eyes. ❧

6

Directly Experiencing Life

For the past few chapters we have been strengthening the muscle of your attention, inviting you to be curious about your breath, your storyteller, and your body. It is now time to bring your awakening curiosity into what is happening as you move through your day. This is where it all gets very interesting. Rather than Life being a random series of events that are happening either because you are doing it right or doing it wrong, you begin to trust that Life is putting you in the exact situations that are needed to bring up the spells that make up your clouds. This way you can see them in operation. In that powerful moment of just "knowticing" them, they lose their power over you.

I like to say it this way:

Life is set up
to bring up
what has been bound up,
so it can open up
to be freed up,
so you can show up
for Life.

In other words, Life is for you. Another way to say it is "what's in the way *is* the way." Any experience that tightens you has been set up by Life to bring up what has been bound up inside so that these parts of yourself can open to the light of your curiosity. As they open, they move through you rather than being stuck inside, where they cause all sorts of difficulties in your life. The more you free what has been bound up, the more your clouds thin and the more available you are to Life.

Rather than trusting Life enough that you show up for what it is offering you, you have been conditioned to resist what you are experiencing. You are in a tug-of-war with your own experience, and this has prevented you from recognizing the field of well-being that is always there. To not resist what you are experiencing is to let go of your end of the tug-of-war rope so that you can bring the healing power of your own curiosity to what you are experiencing.

Though the storyteller is seductive and seems very strong, it is not stronger than your ability to see it and unhook from its stories. One of the core stories to recognize is the belief that you need to change your inner or outer environment in order to know the peace and well-being you long for. Nothing could be further from the truth. Nothing needs to be changed. The stories of struggle need to be seen for what they are: narratives in your head that you became lost in when you were young.

Think of a time when a major problem in your life was suddenly solved. Can you remember how light and energized you became? It was as if a hundred-pound weight had been lifted from your heart. That weight is your storyteller, who keeps on creating problems and contracting around its struggles. Through curiosity, you can learn to unhook from the stories as they are happening, no matter what occurs in your life. As you unhook from your storyteller, you discover the meadow of well-being that is always with you.

❊ Allow one long, deep in-breath and say the sound *Ahh* as you are breathing out. ❊

THE YOU-TURN

In learning how to show up for what Life offers, it helps to become what I call a "tightness detective." Whenever you identify with the spells that make up your clouds of struggle, your body, heart, and mind tighten. This dims the free-flowing aliveness that you are. Tightness signals you to become curious about what you are expe riencing. Whenever you are tightening, it is guaranteed that you are resisting something, so you need to become alert to the times you tighten. Rather than getting lost in all the stories running through your head, you turn toward your experience, giving your stories the acknowledgment they need to begin to open again.

Let's say you are at work and your boss is upset with you about something you haven't done. In the past, you may have fallen into a story of "I'm not smart enough." Or you thought, "He is a horrible boss." You may have reacted by becoming immobile like a deer in headlights, or by arguing with your boss. You may have believed the criticism and judged yourself unmercifully. All of these reactions keep what was triggered stuck inside you. But now, after your boss leaves, you notice that your neck and stomach feel tight. Instead of being a victim of the experience and distracting yourself, you find the willingness to be curious instead. I call this willingness to be curious a *you-turn* because just as you reverse direction with a U-turn while driving, you change your direction from focusing on people and experiences "out there" to being curious about what an experience brings up inside.

When faced with something uncomfortable, most people spend their energy reacting, blaming, fixing, or running away. But these responses never heal anything in the long run. It is a gigantic leap in your awakening when you realize that your suffering does not come from what is happening in your life. *Suffering comes from believing your stories about what is happening.* People who have gone through great suffering and emerged empowered did so because they were able to make a you-turn—they noticed when they were getting tight and they didn't get hooked into the stories of victimhood. In   showed up for what Life was giving them.

A good friend who had been applying the you-turn to little upsets in her life told me of a time when she and her husband had a very heated argument. In the middle of it she was caught in her spells. The feeling of being a victim was there, along with the urge to attack him. But her reactions woke up her curiosity, and she excused herself. She went into another room, sat quietly, and simply watched her story-teller go wild with stories. One moment the storyteller made a list of all the reasons she should leave her husband. In the next moment the storyteller was afraid he would leave her. My friend didn't buy into any of these stories. Instead she just watched them, and slowly the stories wound down. Afterward, she and her husband were able to communicate clearly.

It does take time to unhook at the level that she did, but that is the power of the you-turn. It brings your attention back to yourself, espe-cially when you find yourself getting tight, so that you can recognize your stories and the sensations and feelings they generate. It is when you can see what is going on inside of you that you can give these parts the attention they need to let go. It is a given that if you are tightening, there is a spell that is activated and needs your attention. Every time you turn your attention toward what you are experiencing, your clouds of struggle thin, and it becomes easier to connect with the meadow of your being.

{ Dip the finger of your attention into the river of
your experience and simply notice what you notice.
This moment matters. }

THE WISDOM OF YOUR BODY
You spent time exploring your body in the last chapter because the body is your GPS system for Life. If you listen, it will tell you exactly what is going on inside of you. Every single story and the feelings it generates are expressed in your body in a particular way, and your body will signal you, long before your mind will, that you are reacting to something. You may notice that your heart is pounding or there is a lump in your throat—or maybe a fist in your solar plexus. You might

also notice a cramp in your neck, a heavy weight on your chest, or a hollow feeling in your belly.

All these physical reactions are manifestations of the stories and feelings that were awakened through a particular encounter. Every pattern of holding in your body is an expression of one of the spells of your storyteller. That cramp in your neck could be an expression of "I didn't do it right." That fist in your stomach might be deep fear that you don't know *how* to do it right. The hollow feeling in your belly could be a manifestation of the fear of being rejected and thus all alone. All of these stories/feelings, which have been with you since you were young, keep showing up in your life because they need to receive the healing of your accepting attention. Your sensations, and the thoughts and feelings that fuel them, are just like you: they want to be heard.

 ❧ Bring your attention to your face and ask yourself, "How do I know I have a face?" In other words, what are the sensations happening right now in your face? Are there tingles there? Maybe an itch? Possibly a slight headache? Perhaps some pressure? Find at least three different sensations. When you feel complete, come back to the book. ❧

In these few moments, you were invited to feel what your body was actually experiencing: not an idea about it but the actual, living experience of it. Of course, there may be resistance initially to experiencing your face, for your storyteller is not accustomed to being curious. When I notice that my storyteller has taken over again and is resistant to being curious about what is happening in my body, I tell it, "I know you want to stay in charge, but being present for what is right now is where the good stuff is!" My mind has finally seen that when full attention is brought to my actual experience—especially something I have been resisting—a doorway opens and, with it, the possibility of the bound-up energy releasing. When I remind my storyteller that this is where the good stuff is, it usually lets go, and I can again be fully with whatever is happening right now.

One of the most powerful feedback systems in your body is your belly. When your belly is holding on, it is because you are caught in your storyteller. When you come back to the meadow, your belly automatically softens. If you pay attention, your tight belly will signal that you are believing the stories in your head again. And softening the belly is a gentle reminder to your storyteller that it can let go.

❊ Bring your attention to your belly. Is it soft and open? If it is holding, on the next in-breath tighten it, and then slowly let it go on the out-breath. ❊

If you want to develop the willingness to listen to your body so it can show you the stories that you got caught in, give yourself the gift of noticing your body before you get out of bed each morning. If you honestly ask yourself what you are experiencing, you will discover that you have different sensations every day. One day your shoulder may be cold or your feet hot. Your back may ache one morning and not the next. You may feel rested or tired, hungry or not, peaceful or agitated, contented or anxious. Every moment you actually experience your body is a moment of strengthening your curiosity.

DEEPENING CURIOSITY
It takes time to develop curiosity about what you are actually experiencing, and you may only be able to be this curious about your reactions in situations that don't carry much emotional charge, like during some of your Remembering Sessions. You can also do the you-turn while watching TV or at a movie theater. Be curious about what your storyteller is saying and what kind of sensations and feelings it is generating as you watch the show or film. You can also do this while riding the bus, waiting in line at the post office, or while you're on hold on the phone.

You may be able to bring curiosity into more challenging situations of your life only after you have been triggered. It doesn't matter if it is a couple of hours or a couple of months later. If you revisit the situation after a short delay, the cascades of reactions are still happening and you can bring your attention to them. If it is days, weeks, or months later, you can go back in your imagination and meet with your attention what is brought up inside of you. The more you do this, the more you will be able to summon your curiosity immediately after a challenging situation, and then right in the middle of one. That is freedom.

To sharpen your curiosity at different moments throughout your day, ask yourself, "What is my storyteller saying right now?" At first you may not notice anything because, like most people, you have been lost inside your storyteller for most of your life. At the beginning, asking what your storyteller is saying can feel like asking somebody to describe something they have never seen. But keep on asking anyway. That level of curiosity will begin to open doors that allow you to step outside of the house of your storyteller and learn to relate to what it is saying, rather than from it.

If the question "What is my storyteller saying right now?" doesn't call to you, here are some others that will invite you into the healing of a you-turn:

- What is tightening in my body right now?
- What can I notice about my immediate experience?
- What is sitting here right now?
- What is showing up right now?

Remember, with this kind of question you are not trying to find an answer with your mind, make something go away, or change anything. You are using it to wake up your curiosity so that your attention and your immediate experience can meet. That is where alchemy happens. When you notice something—a sensation, a story, or a feeling—name it. This is what you were doing in the Week 4 Remembering Session when you named whether you were drifting off into the past or the future.

The most basic naming is "Story." But as you develop your capacity to see what is going on, you will be able to be more specific about what you see—fear, sadness, planning, spacing out, irritation, boredom, to name a few. At the beginning you may be confused about exactly what you are experiencing. So confusion is what you are experiencing, and you can then say, "Confusion!"

When you name something, you are relating to what you are experiencing rather than being caught in it or resisting it. This is a moment of freedom, and each moment of freedom counts. For most people, being identified with their storyteller is like being in a wind tunnel with their various spells—pieces of their individual puzzle—flying all around. At moments you may be happy about floating around, but then a puzzle piece hits you in the eye, and it hurts! Or the force of the wind slams you against the side of the tunnel. Not much fun. You are being shown that you don't have to stay in the wind tunnel of your mind. Through curiosity, you can step out of it and then discover how to stick your hand back into the tunnel to grab a piece of the puzzle here and there.

Naming whatever you are experiencing is like looking at the piece of the puzzle you have taken out of the wind tunnel and then putting it on the table in front of you. Every moment of seeing and naming what you are actually experiencing is another step in assembling the puzzle. You may not be able yet to see where a piece fits in the puzzle, but that will become clearer as you deepen your ability to be curious. Slowly, piece by piece, the entire picture of your storyteller becomes apparent, and you can clearly see the spells upon which your storyteller bases its world of struggle. In that clarity, whatever pattern you are noticing won't have as much power to draw you back into the storyteller's wind tunnel.

As you learn how to experience directly what you are experiencing, know that resistance will be a part of it. In fact, you could say that resistance lies at the core of your clouds of struggle. You have spent most of your life resisting your experience. Your mind may want to argue with that, but if you look closely, you will see that mostly you want your experience to be different than what it is rather than the real thing.

Resistance is all about getting as far away from your experience as you can, for your storyteller wants to stay in control by not looking at it. No need to judge or fight that. You, and everyone else, learned very early in life that the only way you could stop being overwhelmed by painful experiences was to resist them by tightening your body, holding your breath, and not looking. This caused you to retreat to your mind and, for most of your life, to unconsciously resist anything that is confusing, uncomfortable, or scary, which only kept you lost in the spells of your storyteller.

But you no longer have to get lost in resistance, and *you don't have to resist your resistance.* Instead you can have a direct experience of it. Like all feelings, resistance has a story, along with an emotional component that is unique, and it shows up in your body in a particular way. However you notice it, acknowledge that it is here. Then you can ask the resistance, "What is it that you are taking care of?" If something reveals itself, great. If not, then continue on with your life, remembering that this kind of question sets things in motion, and Life will show you what is asking to be seen when you are ready for it.

⊰ Pause for a moment and ask, "What is my storyteller saying right now?" Name whatever you notice. If you are not clear, say "Story" and then return to reading. ⊱

DISCOMFORT

To be fully awake to Life means showing up for both the easy and the difficult, the joyous and the sorrowful. The truth is, being open to Life means experiencing pain. It hurts to break your leg or get the flu or stub your toe. And everybody you love will die before you, or you will die before them.

If you are like most people, you're happy to show up during easy situations, but you are not at all comfortable with being curious about even slightly difficult situations. It is important to understand that you turn your pain into suffering when you resist it. In fact, it is in discomfort that you most often leave yourself for the world of struggle. So it could be said that you abandon yourself when you most need yourself.

To discover the transformative power of bringing together your attention and your immediate experience, you need to change your relationship with discomfort. It becomes a lot easier to stay open to Life when you learn how not to tighten around discomfort; that only increases your clouds of struggle. Softening around discomfort—physical, mental, or emotional—allows it to pass through you much more quickly.

Many things in life can evoke discomfort: illness, traffic jams, rejection, irritation, financial challenges, pain in your back, anxiety, big thighs, loss, shame. Every day you are either feeling discomfort or trying to get away from it.

We carry around so much pain. First, our bodies usually are experiencing some discomfort somewhere. When you begin checking into your body, you will be amazed at how much chronic tightness you carry all day long.

My niece, naturopathic doctor Jody Stanislaw, wrote about her experience with chronic tension during a ten-day silent meditation retreat, which she describes in her book *Hunger: An Adventurous Journey of Finding Peace Within*. During morning meditation on day eight, she was supposed to be doing a body scan. Instead, her body began to spontaneously move. Part of her thought she should stop these movements and get back to practicing the meditation technique, but she made the choice to allow the movement to happen, enjoying seeing where and how her body wanted to move. She said it felt as if her muscles were literally unwinding. After the meditation, she clasped her arms behind her back and raised them in the air, something she had never been able to do. Not even an inch. And now she could raise them to a ninety-degree angle.

Jody wrote, "I was amazed to realize it had taken me over a week of stillness and meditation for my muscles to fully let go. It made me acutely aware of how much tension I must hold on a daily basis. My back felt phenomenal. It was more supple and relaxed than I could ever remember it being before. I pondered how contracted we humans can be, not just physically, but mentally, too. I thought about how much suffering we generate when living in this state of self-induced contraction. I became convinced that every time I had resisted or felt pity about a fact of my life, I had created tension in my body, analogous to putting a rock into my metaphysical backpack."

The storyteller also creates tightness in our minds and emotions. There is the background noise of anxiety: "Am I doing this right?" "Will they like me?" "Do I look okay?" "What if I say the wrong thing?" There is also the emotional pain of never being loved enough and having your heart closed to yourself. Finally, there is the disconnect that comes from being lost in your conceptual world and having to think all the time.

It won't take very long in your exploration of your inner life to see that what tightens you is uncomfortable. That is why you have run away from it for so long. Your storyteller's job is to manage your discomfort so you don't have to feel it. But if you look closely, you will see that any attempt to avoid discomfort keeps you bound to it. So you walk around in a low-grade fever of struggle, resisting the healing fever that comes from actually experiencing what you are experiencing. When you remember that fevers are cleansing and you feel better after they pass, you can begin to change your relationship to discomfort. Rather than something to resist, it is something to be with and explore. The more you explore, the more you recognize that discomfort is just trapped energy that needs your full attention in order to be released.

My whole life had been geared around not wanting to feel a very uncomfortable, tightly held ball of yuck in my stomach. I tried to eat it away, drink it away, and numb it away with drugs, but it wouldn't go away, instead influencing many of my actions. When I first started turning toward the ball of yuck with curiosity, it was like looking through thick fog. But slowly I made contact, and lo and behold, as my attention settled there, I found it was nothing to be afraid of. Not only that, but I found that as I gave it my attention, this tightly held energy opened—and there was the peace I had sought for so long by trying to get rid of this feeling.

> ❧ Bring your attention to your belly again. If it is
> tight, there is something you are resisting. Let it
> soften as an invitation to experience whatever you
> are experiencing. ❧

121

THE TREASURES OF DISCOMFORT

If you step back and watch Life unfolding, you can see that it is made out of the opposites of dark and light, and darkness has gotten a bad rap. We are all heat-seeking missiles in search of comfort and pleasure, and we mightily resist any discomfort. Has this ever brought you the peace you long for? If you were honest with yourself, you would say, "Maybe for a little bit here and there, but in the long run, no."

What if you got it backward? What if the treasures of Life that you long for are hidden within the places that you see as uncomfortable? This theme is certainly present in nearly every myth passed down through the ages. The hero always has to go to the places he or she doesn't want to go in order to get the treasure: the princess or the Holy Grail or the pot of gold.

The truth that discomfort is not the black hole you imagined is revealed in the yin-yang symbol, one of the most familiar symbols in the world. It shows the light and the dark nestled together, and there is a point of light in the dark and a point of dark in the light. Each of us is a mix of dark and light, and the people who have unhooked from the game of struggle are those who learned how to change their relationship with the difficult from resistance to curiosity and acceptance.

What would it be like to know that in the uncomfortable challenges of your life there is always a doorway into the light? In other words, your challenges are *for* you. They are not here because you have done something wrong, because someone else has done something wrong, or because the powers-that-be fell asleep on the job. The uncomfortable challenges are fuel for your awakening. As soon as you can embrace the uncomfortable, a door opens inside of you.

What we are talking about here is the theme of "The Guest House," a popular poem by Rumi, a thirteenth-century Persian poet. In this poem, as tr~ lated by Coleman Barks in *The Essential Rumi,* Rumi ͬ all sorts of feelings move through us each day and the ht them. Instead, he says:

Welcome and entertain them all!
Even if they're a crowd of sorrows,

122

who violently sweep your house
empty of its furniture,
still, treat each guest honorably.
He may be clearing you out
for some new delight.
Be grateful for whoever comes,
because each has been sent
as a guide from beyond.

This poem speaks to so many people because it is about the art of alchemy, the power of letting go of resistance and instead opening to experience. Rumi speaks the core truth of consciousness: be grateful for your discomforts because "each has been sent as a guide from beyond." In other words, your discomforts are not here because something is wrong. They are here as your guides through the clouds of struggle and back into the meadow of your being.

The final treasure that comes from the difficulties in your life is that the deepest darkness inside of you, which we all have, can be released through the light of consciousness. Remember, consciousness is the ability to see and be with what is, without needing it to be any different. So your darkness, rather than being a mistake, is Life coming to you in a form that will show you the power of being curious about *what is* rather than the unconsciousness of fixing, changing, judging, getting rid of, or rising above. Your challenges are here to show you that healing isn't about stopping the game of struggle; healing is about exploring it.

TIPS FOR CHANGING YOUR RELATIONSHIP WITH DISCOMFORT

So discomfort is not what it looks like on the surface. The more you open to it, the more you discover an amazing thing: you will always be fine. The only thing that bothers you is your imagined clouds. None of them are solid. They are just clouds passing through the spacious meadow of your being, and you are the awareness that can see what is going on. The more you see what is going on, the more curious you are. The more curious you are about what is happening right now, the more your clouds of struggle thin.

It is important to go slowly. Start with the little ache in your neck or your cold hands. You have resisted discomfort for so long that your inclination is to be afraid of it. So it is important to strengthen the muscle of your curiosity with everyday discomforts that don't have much of a story to them. As your curiosity develops, it will become easier for you to actually be with deep despair, or fiery pain, or even overall agitation, without falling into those experiences or running away as fast as you can.

Also remember that you survived when you were young by numbing yourself to your deepest feelings. And your storyteller was trained to believe that if you open to them again, something bad will happen. Many people have said to me that if they open to their sadness, they will never stop crying. That is just our old fears talking. Yes, if you just feel your sadness, you can get lost in it. But if you discover how to be with it, how to meet it rather than just feel it, you won't get lost and healing will happen.

When you notice you are tightening, it can be very helpful to smile. There is increasing scientific evidence that shows how smiling can literally change the neural pathways in your brain, especially when you allow the smile to fill your body. Many of your reactions will let go in the presence of a smile.

It is also helpful to breathe into the tightening. Remember, as a child you learned how to lessen your feelings by tightening your belly and holding onto your breath. To breathe into an experience allows you to open to it, rather than contract around it. All contraction does is keep this trapped energy bound up inside of you, and there is nothing that is worth closing around. So breathe! In my book *The Gift of Our Compulsions*, there is a wonderful chapter on how to use your breath to open what has been closed. (If you don't have the book, email me at the address at the end of this book, and I will send you the chapter.)

*

It is time to let go of fighting with the difficulties and discomforts of your life. This has only kept you caught in the game of struggle. It is time to learn how to explore your difficulties, understanding that discomfort is pointing you to parts of your storyteller that want to be seen and thinned so you can rediscover the meadow of your natural okayness. You can learn how to honor the difficult aspects of your life. You can experience the magic of turning toward yourself when you get triggered and listening to what is being revealed, giving your reactions the accepting attention they need to transform.

What's in the way *is* the way. Whatever you are experiencing is a doorway into a more spacious place. So rather than resisting discomfort, you can learn how to open to what you are experiencing and explore it without any need to have it be any different than what it is. Being curious about your immediate experience allows your old feelings to pass through you more and more quickly, revealing the meadow of your natural state.

Imagine the absolute joy of not resisting discomfort. Imagine that even in the most difficult situations in your life, your time of reaction is very short before curiosity kicks in, and you feel spacious around whatever you are experiencing. In my life, besides the joy of being open to Life again, the other greatest joy I know is to have a formerly contracted and heavy state come for a visit and not only not be afraid of it, but to turn toward it and be with what I notice. In that moment, I am relating to it rather than from it, and this is what dispels the spells we all took on when we were young.

❦ Find an area of your body where there is holding and bring the light of your attention there. As your curiosity rests there, see what unfolds. Don't force this. You are not trying to make anything happen; you are giving it the accepting attention that allows it to open in its time and in its way. ❧

THE FIVE GREAT TEACHERS
As you go forward with your life, there are five core teachers designed to bring up what most asks for the healing of your attention:

compulsions, illness, pain, finances, and people. Each of these areas is full of invitations to practice the you-turn and to be curious about what they bring up inside you instead of trying to fix, change, or get rid of your experience.

Compulsions

The first teacher is compulsions. We are all compulsive, and you can be compulsive about anything. Whenever you are interested in turning away from yourself through a compulsion, there is a spell close to the surface of your awareness that is asking for the light of your attention. Your compulsion, rather than a problem to be solved, is a guide in showing you what is asking to be seen and released. You can see it and release it through your ability to be very curious, in a spacious and nonjudgmental way, whenever you are interested in overeating, numbing yourself with pills, drinking a whole bottle of wine, or even getting too busy.

This is how I unhooked from my food compulsion. For years I had lost and gained weight many, many times; finally I gained ninety-seven pounds in one year. It slowly dawned on me that trying to control my eating only fueled the compulsion. Instead of always trying to control my urge to eat, I became curious about what I was experiencing when I wanted to turn to food. This was not a quick fix, but it was the way out of the endless game of control, which always resulted in my compulsion controlling me.

When you look at what you are trying to get away from through a compulsion, and when you discover how to give it the light of your attention, the need to be compulsive falls away. Then you are taking care of what you previously tried to address by numbing it.

Illness

Anything out of balance in your body is the body signaling you to pay attention to it, yet most of us were never taught to listen to illness. Instead of being responsible for your experience (which is the ability to respond), you were taught to try to get rid of physical discomfort through pills and surgery. And when that doesn't fully work, you (like most people) tend to numb yourself with food, alcohol, cigarettes, and other ways in an effort to make the discomfort go away.

Pills and surgery do have their place, but most of the body's imbalances come from the ways we attempt to resist what we are experiencing. For example, we drink way too much in order to numb ourselves to our experience, then we wake up the next morning with a lot of self-judgment, a really bad headache, and an unhappy liver. Then we try to get away from this new level of discomfort. This endless game of struggle only brings more dis-ease to our minds and our bodies.

As we discover how to be curious about whatever we experience when we are not feeling well, illness can actually open the door into deep healing. Many of our imbalances can be easily brought back into balance by trusting that Life is inviting us to be with ourselves in a different way.

Pain

The third teacher is the aches and pains you experience. You were taught to contract around both painful feelings and physical pain itself. Over the years, chronic patterns of tightening and holding can turn into painful necks, back spasms, and overly acidic stomachs. If you take the time to explore, with great curiosity, areas of pain in your body, the light of your attention can calm the pain dramatically.

At age twenty-three, I was in a head-on automobile accident. For years afterward, I periodically experienced intense pain in my low back. I tried medical interventions to make it go away, and while they were important, it took me much longer to see that when I was resisting the pain, it amplified. But when I brought the light of my attention to my pain, exploring it with tenderness and mercy, it would calm down.

Pain is what I call a yellow highlighter of life. It underscores areas of holding you took on when you were very young that began as a contraction around a particular spell. For example, that crick in your neck that never wants to go away may very well be expressing the "I am not enough" spell. Or the tight fist in your stomach that comes and goes could be expressing the fear that you are scared of not doing

Life right. When you understand that many patterns of holding that create pain in your body are generated by your spells, the pain will alert you—long before your head does!—that you are lost in a particular spell. Rather than being at the mercy of it, you can explore it.

Finances

How you deal with your finances can teach you much about your fears around being supported by Life and your core mistrust that you will be provided with enough money to survive. Worrying about money is loaded with opportunities to fuel your storyteller and all of its spells. Around finances, fear can spin us into the story "There is not enough." This fear can prod you into constant overwork to make sure you have what you feel is enough. Some people hoard, manipulate, gamble, lie, and even steal to calm this deep belief. Then, if all this controlling and manipulating doesn't work, the storyteller will go into "awfulizing"; it will convince you that something terrible will happen. "There is not enough" is a powerful belief to work with, and it is an invitation to take Rumi's counsel and meet the feelings of fear and dread as guests who have come to bring you the gift of awareness that there is something greater and wiser than you in charge.

People

Some of the most powerful teachers of consciousness are the people in your life: friends, family, lovers, acquaintances, co-workers. On another level, all these people are just character actors in your theater of awakening. They show up at just the right times to bring up what is asking to be seen and released inside you. The people who disturb you most are there to invite you to make a you-turn and work with your reactions.

The more aware you become, the more you realize that you react quite strongly to others when their words and actions wake up one of your spells, especially if a person says or does something you secretly don't like about *yourself*. The more you dislike the part of you that is awakened, the greater your reaction will be, and you can easily sink into the quicksand of blaming, controlling, and defending. On the other hand, the more curious you are about what this person triggers in you, the sooner you will be able to unhook from your reactions.

Bonnie, a woman I counseled, had a boss who seemed angry most of the time because he was so abrupt. This brought up a lot of fear inside of her. As a result, Bonnie was constantly judging him, judging herself, and trying to decide whether she should quit. Needless to say, she was truly struggling. After listening to her, I invited her into the possibility that he was a character actor in her theater of awakening and that she could use her experience with the boss to see and release her own very deep spells.

At first, Bonnie's reactions to what felt like judgment were so strong that she could only notice that she was getting tight. But these were moments of consciousness when she was relating *to* what she was experiencing rather than *from* it. Slowly, as she became curious about what she was experiencing, her body helped her see and meet what interacting with her boss brought up inside of her.

Bonnie noticed that every time she was in his presence or even thought about him, her stomach would tighten in a knot. When she brought her attention to this knot and listened to it, she met the very deep fear that she is not now and never will be good enough. When she was able to bring compassionate attention to this knot in her stomach, it relaxed and she was then able to return to her center more quickly.

This empowered Bonnie so much that she stayed with her job and used her boss to highlight patterns of reaction and contraction that needed her attention. And the wonderful thing is that, as she pulled herself out of reaction and into meeting herself with compassion, she experienced her boss as being a much nicer man! This supports the truth that as we heal our inner world, it changes our experience of the outer world!

*

Learning the art of the you-turn is a huge step in being responsible for your own experience. You begin to realize that most of what you experience regarding compulsions, illness, pain, finances, and people is just your clouds, which arise from the spells you took on. In the past when you were triggered by experiences in your life, you fell into victim mode. The more often you can make a you-turn and become interested in what arises inside you, the less reactive you are and the more quickly your reaction passes, opening you again to the spaciousness of your heart.

> ❊ Bring forth into your imagination one of the core challenges you are experiencing at this time in your life. Open to the possibility that this challenge is *for* you. Ask Life, "What are the treasures embedded in this challenge?" Then let that question work its magic. ❊

CURIOSITY AND YOUR DAILY LIFE
In the last two chapters, we have been exploring the phenomenal power of your own focused attention and how it will help you see the clouds in your mind and then see through them so you can recognize the meadow of your being again. I hope you have been able to see that ignorance is not bliss. In fact, avoiding looking just keeps you caught in the world of struggle, cut off from the joy of being fully alive.

I invite you not to make curiosity another task to do in your life. That is just more of the same old system of your mind trying to *do* Life and do it right. Instead, I invite you to wake up each morning with a simple willingness to be curious. Be willing to experience directly what you are experiencing by being honest with yourself. Be willing to gift yourself with your Remembering Session every day. Now is the time for you to take responsibility for your own inner world rather than getting lost in reaction, blame, shame, resistance, and fear. You have the choice to be curious about what is tight inside of you or to continue trying to avoid it.

To deepen curiosity in your daily life, write down some of the questions we explored previously and put these little reminders in places where you will come across them numerous times throughout the day. In your wallet, on the dashboard of your car, on the bathroom mirror, on your TV. Ask these questions when you're sitting at a stoplight or eating breakfast or sitting at the computer. The more you dip the finger of your attention into the river of your experience, the more the muscle of your curiosity will strengthen. Then you will be able to live these questions when you notice you are tightening around an experience. Eventually you will be able to access curiosity no matter what is happening in your life.

The more you invite yourself to be curious, the less resistant you become to whatever you are experiencing. You will no longer be afraid of what Life may bring you because you know that even the challenges are *for* you, bringing up whatever is asking for healing. You then live Life in a state of discovery, opening to the adventure of Life.

Yes, this takes courage, but know that the root word for *courage* is from Old French, meaning "of the heart." Yes, you have been trained your whole life not to experience what you are experiencing. But I ask you: Do you want all of the bound-up pain to remain stuck inside you? Or as Pema Chödrön wrote in her book *The Places That Scare You:* "Do I prefer to grow up and relate to life directly, or do I choose to live and die in fear?"

Transformation doesn't happen overnight. What we are exploring here is the journey of a lifetime. But what is more important than coming back to yourself, becoming yourself, and giving Life the gift of being fully you? Every moment you go toward your experience rather than getting lost in it or running away from it clears more of your clouds of struggle so you can be fully alive.

As you are developing your curiosity, you may notice that a lot of things don't let go easily. In the next chapter we will explore the art of listening. The deepest parts of your story of struggle need to be touched by an accepting heart. As they receive the power of being listened to and welcomed, true alchemy happens.

KEY POINTS

- Life is set up to bring up what has been bound up, so it can open up to be freed up, so you can show up for Life.

- Freeing up what has been bound up is about showing up for your life rather than always trying to make it be what you think it should be.

- Whenever you are identified with the spells that make up your clouds, you tighten. Your body, heart, and mind tighten, dimming the free-flowing aliveness that you are.

- Become a tightness detective. Instead of being upset about being upset, become curious.

- When triggered, most people react, blame, fix, or run away, which never heals anything. The you-turn is bringing your attention back to you so that you can recognize the stories, sensations, and feelings that are asking for the attention they need to let go.

- Every single feeling you have is expressed in your body in a particular way, and your body will signal you long before your mind will that you are reacting to something.

- Ask yourself, "Do I really want my reactions running my life?"

- Know that resistance will be a part of directly experiencing what you are experiencing. You have spent most of your life resisting your immediate experience.

- By not tightening around discomfort, you allow the clouds of struggle to pass through you.

- Your discomforts are not here because something is wrong. They are here as your guide through the clouds of struggle and back into the meadow of your being.

- Now is the time to stop fighting with the difficulties and discomforts of your life and to learn how to explore them, understanding that discomfort is a doorway.

- Ask yourself, "Do I prefer to grow up and relate to Life directly, or do I choose to live and die in fear?"

-

-

-

> REMEMBERING   Week 6
> This week's Remembering Statement:
> *What story am I listening to right now?*
> Your own statement:

Remembering Session

We have been developing the muscle of your attention by bringing it first to your breath, and from this foundation, having you become curious about what your storyteller is doing (past and future). We then invited your attention into the GPS of your body, which will signal you, through how it tightens and holds, when you are struggling with the clouds in your mind. This week you will develop the capacity to meet whatever you are experiencing with the compassionate curiosity it needs to be released.

There are two phrases we will add at the end of your calming/focusing words: "As is . . . I'm here." These words invite both your attention and your heart to be with whatever you are experiencing. So you will silently say with the rhythm of your breath, "In . . . out. Deep . . . slow. Calm . . . ease. As is . . . I'm here." (Or you can say just the new words on their own.)

Saying "As is" on your in-breath reminds you of the willingness to allow yourself to be exactly as you are in this moment. It reminds you of the art of letting go of struggling with whatever is (your usual mode) so that you can move into the place of healing that comes from allowing yourself to be exactly as you are. If you open to the depth of "As is," your belly will soften and your mind will become very curious about what is happening inside of you.

Saying "I'm here" on your out-breath reminds you to be with whatever Life is offering you in this moment. It reminds you to be keenly attentive to what is, in a way that invites your heart to be open to the parts of you that are asking to be seen. Remember, attention heals. The parts of you that keep on taking you away from the circle of your breath need somebody to be with them, just like a child does, so they can let go. Just imagine how it feels when you are hurting and somebody says, "I am here with you. Tell me about it." Then you will know the healing power of "I'm here."

Putting together these two statements reminds you of the healing power of your heart. Saying them with the rhythm of your breath invites you to move beyond the endless struggle of trying to be who you think you should be and allows you to embrace all parts of your being. When you do, you can receive the nourishment of compassionate attention from the only source that really matters: you. As you soften around your experience—as you allow it to be here and even welcome it—it will open up in its own time, and the energy that was bound up in it will expand and release.

After you read the following section, put down the book, close your eyes, and begin exploring. If you are timing your session, add one minute to the previous week's session for a total of ten minutes. If time is not an issue, stay with each step as long as your curiosity is engaged.

Let's begin:

❊ Close your eyes and dip the finger of your attention into the river of your experience, noticing what it is like to be you right now.

For at least three in-breaths, tighten your muscles, and then very slowly relax everything on your out-breath as you say the great sound of letting go, *Ahh!*

Bring your attention to the circle of your breath, saying the calming/focusing words, "In . . . out. Deep . . . slow. Calm . . . ease."

Now add "As is" on the in-breath and "I'm here" on the out-breath to the calming/focusing words. (Or you can say "As is . . . I'm here" alone for this session.) Allow yourself to feel the kind of relationship with yourself that these words are pointing to. When you notice a story, a sensation, or emotion capturing your attention or taking you away from the circle of your breath, allow "As is . . . I'm here" to remind you to be open to the experience. Be as welcoming as you can about whatever is arising and then return to your breath, allowing the calming/focusing words to remind you to be with yourself in an attentive and spacious way.

Stay with this as long as it interests you, grounding with your breath and the calming/focusing words, watching things grab your attention and giving them the power of your own accepting attention. When you are done exploring (it may be a few seconds or a few minutes), return to the circle of your breath.

At the end, expand your awareness and be curious about your experience after having given yourself the gift of your own attention.

When you are ready, open your eyes. ☙

Abbreviated Version

❧ Close your eyes and check in, noticing what it is like to be you right now.

For at least three in-breaths, tighten your muscles, and then very slowly relax everything on your out-breath as you say the great sound of letting go, *Ahh!*

Bring your attention to the circle of your breath, saying the calming/focusing words, "In . . . out. Deep . . . slow. Calm . . . ease. As is . . . I'm here." (Or you can say "As is . . . I'm here" by itself.)

If you notice a story, sensation, or emotion that is capturing your attention or taking you away from the circle of your breath, allow the essence of "As is . . . I'm here" to remind you to meet it in an open and spacious way. Then bring your attention back to the circle of your breath and the calming/focusing words.

At the end, expand your awareness and be curious about your experience after having given yourself the gift of your own attention.

When you are ready, open your eyes. ☙

7

All Is Welcome Here

In the last two chapters we developed the muscle of your attention so you could become curious about whatever you are experiencing right now. Through curiosity, you can learn to unhook from many of your spells and allow them simply to pass through you. But the more you turn your attention within, the more you will see that there are some very tightly held parts of you that won't let go when you bring your attention to them. You also need to listen to them and to listen from your heart.

Many of us are afraid to do this because what we hear is often disturbing and confusing. And yet to be fully open to Life, we need to be open to whatever is going on inside. There is a whole host of characters within you—arrogance, despair, righteousness, helplessness, judgment, entitlement, revenge, self-pity—that you don't want anybody else to know is there. There is no need to be ashamed of these characters; everybody has them. When they don't let go under the light of your curiosity, they need to be listened to. When they are heard, they cease to have power over you.

It is your heart that can approach them, listen to their view of the world, and thus release them from the prison of your resistance to them. When I talk about the heart, I am talking about the energy center in your chest that is open to Life. Whereas your mind is dualistic in nature, caught up most of the time in liking/disliking and wanting/resisting, the energy in your chest is a lover of what is. It includes rather than excludes. It accepts rather than rejects. Your heart trusts rather than fears, and it weaves every single part of you and every single part of your life back into the whole that it truly is.

When you were young, your heart center was open. Life was something you felt from your heart rather than something you thought about. Rather than needing to control and resist, you saw Life as magical, fascinating, and full of adventure. But as you got older, you had to shut down your heart. It wasn't safe to keep it open, for it was bruised and hurt by events and people in your life. So you retreated into your head and locked the innocence and healing power of your heart deep inside of you. Keeping the power of your heart locked away takes most of the joy out of Life. Whether you recognize it or not, your deepest longing is to be open to Life again, and it is discovering (or uncovering) your heart that makes this reopening possible.

Let's experience the difference between living from your mind and living from your heart.

❧ Imagine that sitting in front of you is somebody you deeply love (living or dead, person or animal). Remember a time when your heart was completely open to them, and allow your whole being to feel this. If you observe carefully, you will feel that the energy in your chest shifts; it will expand, open, and even glow. If you stay with it long enough, you will experience your whole body glowing.

Now imagine a time when you reacted to your loved one, maybe becoming afraid of losing their love or being angry about something they had done. You will notice that just imagining this event closes the openness in your chest, and the rest of your body also contracts as your mind becomes tight and reactive. This is what happens when your heart becomes closed again. ❧

Which one feels better: the closed, reactive place or the open, loving place? Of course it is the second, for that is who you truly are: an open heart. That place of openness, whose source is in your chest, is the doorway back into the meadow of your natural okayness that is always with you. When it is freed from the clouds of fear and struggle, it becomes vibrantly alive, guiding you every step of the way down the path of Life.

The amazingly wonderful thing is that the storyteller in your head—with its fears, judgments, resistances, doubts, confusions, shame, and addiction to control—is here to teach you about living from your heart again. Everything that tightens you in your life is a request for the healing energy of your heart. The full transformation of the spells that make up your clouds of struggle happens when the spells are met with your compassionate attention. It is your mind that tries to solve things. It is your heart that dissolves them.

Remember, the freedom you're ready for doesn't come from changing anything. It comes from the ability to see and be with what is right now. When you are caught in your mind, you try to fix, change, and get away from whatever you are experiencing. When your heart begins to open again, you discover the healing of not resisting what you are experiencing. This discovery brings you to the phenomenal healing power of "all is welcome here," which is the opposite of resisting. When you resist, you empower what you are resisting, but when you welcome your immediate experience—especially when you stay open around what has been closed inside of you—your spells lose their power over you.

✧ Take a moment to wake up your heart center by repeatedly tapping your chest and smiling. ✧

TOUCHING YOURSELF WITH YOUR OWN HEART
At times you may be able to give your close friends and loved ones the spaciousness of your heart, but you, like most people, are probably unskilled at giving this amazing nourishment to yourself. Instead, you have been conditioned to fix, judge, ignore, deny, or try to understand

what you are experiencing, which is the ultimate seduction, and all of this keeps you caught in your head.

If you stop and truly listen to what you are experiencing in any given moment, you will see that you have a community inside that's made up of a cast of characters that has been with you since you were young. (Carl Jung was one of the first people who presented the idea that each one of us is made up of a community of parts.) And if you were honest with yourself, you would see that there are many parts of you that you have locked out of your own heart.

You were conditioned to believe that if you ignored the disliked parts they would go away, so you kept them stuffed inside by staying very busy, watching endless TV, eating, drinking, shopping, or texting. It is startling to realize that when you ignore these parts, they influence you from beneath your everyday awareness, which is much like having young children in charge of your life. (Just think about the last argument you were caught in and the things you said—and how you said them—and you will see how young these parts are.)

To know the aliveness that you long for, every part of you needs to be woven back into your heart. The deep fears, angers, self-judgments, and despairs that are hidden inside you have been with you since you were little, and just like you, they want to be seen, acknowledged, understood, and loved so they can let go.

Why is it so powerful to be curious and accepting about what you are experiencing rather than trying to change it in any way? Attention that is accepting heals. One of the most powerful paradoxes you will come across on your healing journey is that true transformation can only happen in an atmosphere of acceptance and listening. When you give accepting attention to whatever you are experiencing, the energy that was bound up in it begins to expand, move, and eventually let go.

Imagine having a bad day and sharing it with a friend who, instead of listening to you, tries to fix you, judges you, or ignores you. What feelings does that bring up? They're probably not very pleasant. Now imagine that your friend really listens to you from his or her heart, and rather than judging or trying to fix you, your friend accepts you. The chances are you would feel a lot lighter after being listened to in this way because you were given the spaciousness to experience what you were experiencing.

A wonderful example of bringing this kind of listening to ourselves comes from Krista, a young woman who I have been coaching:

> My boyfriend and I had gone downtown to meet up with some friends. After a few hours, I got hungry and wanted to go home to make dinner. Sensing that he wanted to stay out longer, I hesitatingly asked if he wanted to come home and eat with me or hang out for a while. He told me he wanted to hang out longer, but he would give me a ride home. As we walked to the car, I could feel it all building up—the voices in my head started their familiar banter of "I'm not fun enough," "What's wrong with me?" and "I don't deserve him." My stomach tightened into a fist. My throat grew into a hard ball of mucus, and the space around my heart began to close. All this buildup was so familiar that it carried with it a false sense of security and comfort. It carried with it a spell that had been cast long ago.
>
> As we drove home, I started to notice something shift in me. I not only realized, but also really saw, that I was the one watching this story unfold. I was not the story itself. I could feel the story holding on as if its life depended on it. It did not want to let go. And then I recalled something I had read earlier that week about the power of shifting your perspective when the spells arise. I began to thank all the voices, all the intense energy within, and instead of resisting, I smiled at them, being grateful that they were coming up. I felt my heart open and release as my perspective shifted. I kept repeating to myself, "I allow my heart to be open; I allow all of this to move through my open heart."
>
> It was incredible! My body started to soften, my mind calmed down, and for the rest of the ride home, we laughed and smiled and expressed our deep love for one another. It was a revelation for me. By opening my heart to this experience, I was able to see it for what it was: a spell that wanted to be healed, a spell that needed my attention, a spell that deserved

compassion and kindness, a spell that showed up to open me to the love and healing power within.

❮ For a few minutes, breathe in and out of your heart. Then ride the waves of your breath, saying silently to yourself, "As is . . . I'm here." Meet yourself exactly as you are. ❯

EVERYTHING LONGS FOR THE HEART

Why have you not fully met yourself with your own heart? Because you were trained (by your parents, teachers, peers, and society) to believe that you aren't okay the way you are and need to be fixed. Fixing is just the endless game of your storyteller and comes from being taught to judge and fear what goes on inside of you. Remember, there is nothing inside to be ashamed of or afraid of. These beliefs were just conditioned into you, and when you finally look at them, they are no more substantial than a cloud. Also, we're all nutty as fruitcakes, so the parts you have hidden deep inside because of fear and shame, everybody else has, too.

Instead of seeing yourself as someone who has unacceptable parts that need to be fixed (and thus becoming a victim to your life), you just need the power of an aware heart. In order to access the full power of your own heart, it helps to recognize that your wounded parts have been given to you by Life to teach you about the power of accepting attention. You don't have these parts because your parents screwed you up or because God fell asleep on the job. There is nobody to blame. Your parents, teachers, siblings, and peers were just the delivery system of the wounds that you took on, and these wounds are here to teach you about opening your heart.

Rather than being a victim to these so-called unacceptable parts of yourself, you begin to see that the spells you took on when you were very young are the doorway back into the meadow. They are the raw material of your awakening, and when you resist them, your clouds of struggle only get denser. When you bring these parts home to your heart, your clouds thin, and joy and aliveness that are Life emerge. For in the long run, the only thing that truly heals is Love, and Life will put you in the situations you need for bringing up the parts that need your heart's acceptance.

There is a woman in one of my counseling groups, Cynthia, who was unknowingly and deeply betrayed by her boyfriend right before they broke up. A month after the breakup, he told her he just tested positive for HIV. She came to group a few hours after he told her and a few hours before she herself got tested. Words cannot describe how amazing that group was—human beings open to what was showing up inside all of them and meeting it all in their hearts. Later that afternoon, Cynthia's first test came back negative, but she had two more to go. In the middle of this, she emailed the following to the entire group:

> I wanted to tell you again how grateful I am for your love and for how preciously you have been holding the space for me in this cracking-open that Life is giving me. I continue to be amazed at how I am showing up for this process and at how much is being revealed and delighted within me through opening to this experience. I fully understand what Mary means when she says there is no part of myself that does not deserve my loving attention, and there is nothing worth closing around.
>
> This doesn't mean there haven't been waves of grief, sadness, anger, and terror, but they have passed through quickly as I've softened into them and allowed them the space to be here. Last night resistance showed up, and I spent the hours from 10:00 p.m. to 3:00 a.m. working with it, not closing it out of my heart.
>
> When I was in resistance, the picture of being in an inflatable raft in full-body armor on a raging river, with huge rocks jutting out from every angle, came to me. When I resist what I'm experiencing, I desperately try to stay clear of the rocks, fighting a losing battle as water capsizes my boat and it begins to deflate. Not a fun or enjoyable experience. But when I open my heart and allow whatever I am experiencing to be as it is, it is as if I am in that raft, in my swimsuit, lounging and soaking up the sun, delighting in the waves and the turns, and feeling the exhilaration of the river carrying me safely on my way.

What a difference a small shift in my thinking makes—from resistance to "I am right where I need to be," "Life is supporting me," "I am being carried down this river," and "I can let go and trust that I am safe." I wanted to share this with you all because there are so many smaller challenges that I once thought it impossible to turn toward. Now I know without a doubt that if I can do this, with the possibility of HIV and everything else that goes with this challenge, there is not one thing that I cannot hold in my heart and eventually love. I know this to be true for all of you as well, and so I am holding this space for you in whatever is showing up in your life today.

What would it be like to realize that all your painful feelings are just frozen energy that is asking for love? What would your life look like if you realized that the energy that is bound up inside of you truly will loosen when touched by acceptance? Most of the time, you just want your spells and the discomfort that they generate to go away. What your feelings want is your heart, and they will keep on showing up until they receive the lasting healing of your accepting attention.

❧ Take a moment and gently rest a hand on your chest. Feel your heart beating and your breath rising and falling. Can you allow yourself to be exactly where you are right now? Can you give yourself a smile? ❧

I SEE YOU

You are now ready to give your spells the accepting attention they need in order to let go. Before you do this, it is important to remember two core truths we have been exploring throughout the book.

The first is that your pain is made worse by your resistance to it. In fact, your resistance turns your pain into suffering. This is true for physical, mental, and emotional pain. What a joy it is to discover that when you stop resisting what you are experiencing and touch it with your heart, not only does it become more bearable, it has a tendency to pass through you much more quickly.

The second truth is that the spells you have bought into your whole life are not you. They are just conditioned states that keep you separate from the meadow of your being. They can be seen and seen through. And they aren't even yours: they are ours, for all human beings take on these spells. It is a wonderful moment when, caught in a spell, you recognize that other people, right at that exact time, are lost in that story, too.

These two truths will help you develop your capacity to turn toward your experience. As you do, you will be able to see that the spells show up as clouds of stories in your head that generate sensations and feelings in your body.

Let's take anger for example. It may show up as a tight fist around your stomach. If you look carefully, you will see the story that generates that fist. It may be saying, "They did it wrong" or "I am going to make them pay." It also has an emotional component, and the feeling of anger is energetically different than any other feeling. Whether you notice the reactions of your clouds as they express in your body, how they talk in your head, or how they feel, every moment of "knowticing" makes a difference.

There is a very simple but profound way to bring the power of accepting attention to what you are experiencing. It is through saying "I see you" to whatever you are noticing. This allows you to access the healing power of the you-turn. When you say "I see you," your attention and your immediate experience come closer together, opening the possibility that the holding you are experiencing can begin to soften with the help of your "knowticing." (You may find that saying "I see you" is too much for some parts that were frozen at a very early age. They may be too scared to come out of hiding even though they really want to be seen. If so, try saying, "I acknowledge that you are here.")

Every moment of saying "I see you" is a moment of consciousness. Over time, as you develop the muscle of your curiosity, you will be able to bring the healing of compassionate curiosity and accepting attention to whatever is happening in your life. Then you will be able to see that your old reactions want to be released. They want to be able simply to pass through you without you getting caught in their stories.

The pull to get trapped in your reactions to your clouds is very strong. A good example comes from a friendship of mine. I noticed that the only time my friend and I connected was when I called. Then there came a time when he wouldn't return my calls. I reached him one day and asked how he was doing, and he said he was fine, but busy. I then shared with him the feelings that came up for me when he didn't return my calls. He said he understood, but he still didn't respond to my calls. I finally stopped calling, and when I thought of him, I would often feel either anger (and think, "He is wrong") or self-judgment (and think, "What did I do wrong?"), which is just anger turned within.

It was very seductive to stay with my anger, but I was awake enough to know this was an opportunity to be with some bound-up energy inside of me. When the anger came up, I would turn my attention to where it was expressing itself in my body and give it my attention, letting it know "I see you."

As I met the anger, it would step aside and reveal a deep sadness in my belly. I could see how young it was and how this was a core experience of my childhood. (My father, with whom I lived for the first twelve years of my life, had completely ignored me because I was not the boy he had wanted.) I could also see how much of my life was about trying to get away from this painful feeling of not mattering, which had frozen in my belly. Finally, this feeling was mattering to me, and I was giving it the recognition it needed in order to let go.

❴ What's happening in your belly right now? ❵

So through this friendship, Life was setting me up to confront this bound-up feeling of despair that I had buried in my belly long ago. Rather than staying caught in the story of anger, I turned toward my experience, and through the light of my accepting attention and the power of telling it "I see you," it opened up and thawed out. (Remember, this is just frozen energy that longs to be released.) Because I was no longer holding it inside of me through my resistance to it, it was freed up to move right through me. That is the power of attention.

Through meeting my anger, I realized how much the feeling of not mattering had influenced my life, putting a wall between me and Life. Now that I can be present with it, I am much more able to show up fully for Life. Before, when this feeling was triggered, I would be silently angry and then try to shut the person out of my life and withdraw because my anger brought up this old pain. Now that I am no longer afraid of this feeling, it is much easier to accept people as they are. If it looks to me as though someone is ignoring me or rejecting me, I do the you-turn and acknowledge what this perception brings up inside of me instead of projecting the responsibility for my feeling onto them. Now I am grateful when an old feeling rises to the surface so that I can give it the attention it needs simply to pass through me.

All the deep feelings inside of us are just energy that got trapped in spells and bound up in our bodies. And, like all energy, they want to move. They want to be set free. When you find yourself in a situation where your old reactions surface, you can help them move through you by taking a walk, enjoying a shower, or talking to a friend. But that just temporarily moves them. What they need to be set free is your accepting attention.

STEP BY STEP

To awaken, it is important to know that there is no such thing as an ordinary moment. There are only two kinds of moments: Life is either inviting you to be fully open to Life right here, right now, or it is putting you in the situations that are needed to bring up what has been bound up inside of you so it can open up and be free.

At the beginning, you may only be able to notice that you are struggling. You can then say to yourself, "I see that I am getting tight. There is something inside of me that is asking for my attention." That may not seem like a lot, but it is a moment of consciousness. You can also ask for clarity from the wise Presence that is always with you by asking, "What is asking to be seen?" In chapter 4 we explored the power of asking questions without looking for an answer. We discovered that asking for clarity signals to Life that you want to see what is asking to be transformed, and you then let that request work its magic from beneath your everyday awareness.

It does take courage to turn toward yourself, to give the bound-up energy inside of you the attention it needs to let go. To discover this courage, ask yourself, "Do I really want this feeling running my life?" You are only alive for a very short time, and I can assure you that at the end of your life, you won't be celebrating all of the times you got hooked into reaction and fell into your anger, fear, sadness, or shame. Instead, you will be oh so grateful for developing the ability to unhook from these energy patterns, so that your reactions can simply pass through you, leaving you in touch with the meadow of your natural okayness.

❦ Take a moment now and dip the finger of your attention into the river of experience that is your body. Whatever you notice—maybe a slight headache, contentment in your belly, tightness in your solar plexus, warmth in your feet—let your attention settle there, becoming curious about how energy is expressing itself in that area. To whatever you notice, say, "I see you." ❧

WHAT IT IS LIKE TO LISTEN

We have explored how many spells will simply pass through you when you can see them for what they are: conditioning you took on when you were very young. Let us now explore how to stand with the spells that are so deeply embedded inside of you that they need more than just being seen. They need to be listened to also. As they receive your focused, compassionate listening, these spells that have influenced you your whole life will let go, and you will experience again the meadow of your being that is always with you, right here, right now.

Author Geneen Roth speaks directly to this truth when she says, "Most of our suffering comes from resisting what is already here, particularly our feelings. All any feeling wants is to be welcomed, touched, allowed. It wants attention. It wants kindness. If you treated your feelings with as much love as you treated your dog or your cat or your child, you'd feel as if you were living in heaven every day of your sweet life."

An experience I had at my chiropractor's office speaks to this truth. To understand the depth of the old spells that were awakened inside of me that day, you need to know that a big part of how my story-teller was put together was from a sense that I didn't matter—that my needs were not important and that I didn't have a right even to voice them. For most of my childhood I lived in the same bedroom with an older sister whose survival system was all about being the best. She saw me as "less than," a bother, and she made sure I got the message that she was best at everything. With no one in my world to give me acceptance and affirmation, deep spells were created inside of me, and a couple of the core ones were triggered at the chiropractor's office.

That morning I woke up not feeling well after dealing with an intestinal bug for a few days, but I still needed to see my chiropractor. I usually set aside thirty minutes for the appointment, but I regularly was in and out in about ten minutes. This morning I had already been waiting for twenty minutes when a new person checked in and sat down in the waiting room with me. Five minutes later, he was taken back to see the doctor. When I asked the receptionist why the other patient went back before me, she said she was going to check on it, and then she didn't come back for what seemed like a very long time. When she did, she said, "Yes, we made a mistake." When I responded that I had now been waiting for half an hour and was on a tight schedule, she said she couldn't do anything about it.

I sat down, and immediately what arose inside of me was a lot of anger from the "I must control Life" spell. Life wasn't doing what I wanted it to do, so my storyteller was angry. It is important to know that when a spell gets awakened, like mine was that morning, our reaction is usually irrational in relation to what is going on in the moment. But it is not irrational in relationship to what was frozen inside of us when we were young. So when our frozen feelings get triggered, they show up exactly as they would in childhood. That is why we can have such over-the-top reactions to seemingly inconsequential things.

I was having an over-the-top reaction. My heart was pounding, and I had a knot in my stomach. The stories that were raging through my mind were very childlike and felt very young: "This is not fair." "It was my turn." "I will tell their boss what they did." "They need to be told they were wrong." "I will just get up and leave and show them."

It felt like 99.999 percent of me wanted to run with my reaction, because this experience was super fuel for the reactive righteousness that permeates the "I must control Life" spell. On one level, it felt good to be right, and my storyteller wanted to prove that I had been wronged (a subspell of "I must do it right"). But I was awake enough to know that to give these thoughts energy would only engender more suffering, and I would miss an opportunity to heal some young and wounded parts of myself. Rather than being right, I want to be free.

So the first thing I did was to allow a deep breath of letting go. Then I acknowledged that I was caught. This may not seem like such a big step, but it is. Most people, when Life brings one of their spells up to the surface, simply slip into its story and react from that place, bringing more suffering into their lives. Seeing how tight I had become permitted me to recognize that I was caught in a spell, and this recognition allowed me to take a step back from what I was experiencing.

I then asked Life for clarity. I knew that embedded in every challenge Life gave me was a piece of my puzzle, but I didn't need to figure out on my own what that piece was. I could turn it over to Life, to the Intelligence that was greater than me and always with me. I asked, "What is asking to be met here?"

I then did the you-turn, turning my attention toward my immediate experience. I first went to my body, noticing my stomach was in knots. As I allowed my attention to settle there, I could feel anger radiating like a hot stove from my stomach. I said, "I see you." But this was such a strong reaction in me that it didn't dissipate under the light of just my attention. Instead, it needed the accepting attention of my heart. So I said, "It is okay that you are here."

I had also learned that each part inside of me has its own particular view of the world, and they all respond to being listened to, just as anyone does when they are upset. So I asked this angry one, "Tell me about your world," and simply listened as it told me its story. It raged, blamed, justified, and defended the right to be a victim. I didn't judge it or ignore what it was saying. Instead I let it know I was here with it and that I understood.

I was then able to let it know that it wouldn't be helpful to strike out in anger because that reaction only brings forth more reaction. I also reminded it of all the times in my life that I was able to move out of reaction into responding and how much healing came from that.

Under the light of my accepting attention, the angry one calmed down and let go. I was then able to see the underlying vulnerability that the anger was trying to protect: the feeling that "I don't matter," which is part of the "I am unlovable" spell. I also asked about its view of the world. As it spoke, there was so much sadness, along with the belief that this happened because I was bad (a subspell of the "I am wrong" spell).

It may sound irrational that there was sadness about having my turn taken by another patient, but remember, our reactions to unsettling experiences in our lives are rarely about what is going on right now. They come from the spells we took on when we were little, and they have been waiting our whole lives to be given the attention they need to heal. This feeling of not mattering was one of the core spells I took on, so rather than judging or trying to stop what was going on inside of me, I listened.

When this deep grief felt heard, I was able to say, "You are not alone any more. I have grown up, and I can be with you in the way you needed somebody to be with you when you were young. I'm here now. This didn't happen because you are bad. This happened so you would come close enough to the surface of my awareness and I could meet you with my heart." My whole body began to glow in joy, for in that moment the feeling of not mattering truly mattered to me.

The anger had completely dissipated simply by being heard. The grief calmed down, but a bit of it stayed with me for most of the day, giving me the opportunity to keep meeting it with my heart, to say "I see you. I'm here."

❊ Pause for a moment and turn your attention toward yourself. Whatever you notice (cold feet, a feeling of joy, an anxious mind), say, "I see you. I'm here." ❊

In the beginning of this experience my heart was closed—closed to the receptionist and closed to myself. As I was able to turn toward my experience and give it the light of my attention, I began to soften inside, and my heart began to open. I could feel how young each of these parts was, both the angry one that was trying to protect and the more vulnerable one that felt it didn't matter. I could also see that what both of these were asking for was the same thing I ask for: not to be judged or fixed or ignored, but instead to be seen, heard, and allowed to have their experience. As they felt heard, they let go.

The experience in the chiropractor's office was the culmination of a lifetime of running away from the deep pain of not mattering and then learning how to turn toward it. The pain of this spell was so great when I was young that I had to bury it in order to survive. That didn't make it go away. In fact, I became extremely compulsive in an attempt to run away from this feeling. This spell has also influenced many of the decisions of my life without my ever being aware of it.

It took me years to discover this pathway from the reactive mind to the listening and accepting heart. At first not much seemed to happen, for I didn't yet understand the power of just one moment of bringing my attention and my immediate experience together. But slowly, as I became willing to be honest with myself about what I was experiencing, for a moment here and a moment there, I began to be able to see and listen to the parts of myself that I had hated and feared. When somebody said something that triggered me, I could be curious about my reaction instead of defending myself or making them wrong.

I then learned how to be curious about the tightness in my body that the feelings were generating. Maybe the lump in my throat was the tip of an iceberg of grief, or a tight fist in my stomach signaled the hidden anger of a lifetime. At the beginning I could only notice what was going on in my body for a moment or two before the urge to turn away took over or the sensation seemed to go away. But in those moments, I learned how to say "I see you, and I want to get to know you" without needing anything to happen.

Slowly my spells found the courage to reveal themselves to me. As I let my attention settle into the holdings in my body, these parts would let me see how they experienced the world. I could feel what they were feeling, and I could hear their stories. Because they so deeply longed for the light of my accepting attention, they would eventually find the courage to show themselves fully to me. Now all of my parts are enfolded in my heart.

> ❬ Soften your belly and say to yourself, "All is welcome here." Notice what happens inside of you when you say that. Does the mind resist it, tightening you? Or does it soften your experience, allowing your heart a voice? Or is there maybe a little bit of both? ❭

My experience at the chiropractor's office demonstrates one particular pathway for meeting spells with your heart:

1. I recognized that I was upset.
2. Then I asked Life for clarity.
3. My attention was then naturally drawn toward my immediate experience, and I became curious about what was here.
4. I acknowledged what I was experiencing by saying "I see you."

I used to teach this particular pathway, but I saw many people's storytellers take it over, which only led to frustration. Now I invite people to recognize that the spells inside of them long for exactly what everybody longs for when they want somebody to be there for them: compassionate listening. With that understanding, it will be easier for you to find your own pathway for being present for your spells.

DEEPENING YOUR LISTENING
The pathway described in the previous section is an excellent way to meet most spells with your heart. But the spells we are most afraid of or ashamed of are the ones that need another step. They need you to listen to their world, just as I had in the chiropractor's office. (When you are having a bad day, this type of listening is what you want, too.) This is where you say to whatever you are noticing, "I want to hear about your world."

For many of our deeply frozen spells, it is very important to add, "When you are ready": "When you are ready, I want to hear about your world." Because we have judged them, resisted them, and constantly tried to get rid of them, it takes these spells a while to trust that we truly want to hear about their world. They are like shy fawns who will hide when we try to find them. But they truly want connection, and with patience, they will come out of hiding and let you see them.

Each of your spells has a particular view of the world. They are made up of stories that were created when you were young, and they respond to being heard just like you do. If you are willing to listen, they will tell you about their experience of the world. Your job is to listen, for giving these parts a voice is what allows their bound-up energy to move.

As we explored in chapter 5, there is no need to be ashamed or afraid of what any part tells you. Remember, because these parts were frozen inside of you when you were young, they have the view of a child. They have waited your whole life to be heard, so they can let go under the gaze of your accepting attention. Whether what is asking to be met inside of you shows up as sensations, feelings, or stories, they all just want to be heard.

> ❄ Bring your attention to a familiar place of holding in your body and say to it, "When you are ready, I want to hear how you experience the world." It doesn't matter if anything happens right now. All that matters is your willingness to be curious. When the holding feels safe enough, it will reveal itself to you. ❄

When they are heard, many of your parts will calm down, revealing inside of you the vast space of peace that you really are. But your deepest spells may need the final gift I gave to myself in the chiropractor's office. It is what I call "the invitation." This is when you invite the spell into a perspective that is different from what it has held its whole life. This is what I did with both the angry one and the one that felt it didn't matter. A part that feels it is unlovable may need to hear that you accept it as it is. The part that feels all alone may need to hear that you are there with it, and though at times you may leave, you will come back as soon as you can. It is very important to do this *after* you have listened to the part that is needing to be heard. If you do this before listening, the spell may experience you trying to make it feel different than what it is. After it has been listened to, then there is the possibility that it can open to a new perspective.

One of the most poignant moments in my awakening came as I was working with the part of me that felt that I was bad and wrong to my core. After listening to it, I could see that it needed to hear a different view. So I said, "We have turned out to be a good person." This part was stunned by this news. It said, "Really?" It had been frozen for so long in the belief that I was bad that it started to cry for the sheer relief of it. It kept on saying, "Is this really true?" And when I would respond "Yes," a fresh wave of tears would come.

Writing down what a spell says can help you to see the world of your spells. Rather than writing paragraphs, I find it is best to write down one-liners. Ask a part how it sees Life, and I assure you, it will be very revealing. My life truly began to open up when I was able to listen to the part inside of me that felt I was a bad person. I had spent most of my life secretly believing this, but also trying to deny it. As I wrote down how this part viewed me, I could see that its perceptions were very young and truly irrational. There were even a few beliefs that this part still wanted to defend as true, such as "You did this when you were twenty-three, and that proves you are bad." This part believed that if I wasn't perfect, then I was bad. But there is no such thing as a perfect person.

Know that only the deepest of spells need this kind of listening and the offer of a different perception. It may take a while before these spells will be able to share with you their view of the world. It takes time to create the kind of relationship that allows them to feel safe enough to be real with you about their world. Also, it is only after they are truly listened to that they will be open to a different view. Just as you calm down and feel much lighter when you are heard, your deep listening allows these very young and hidden parts of you to let go enough for the energy that was bound up in them to be freed.

FINDING YOUR PATHWAY

It is a truly healing moment in your life when you recognize that these spells are not who you are. You are that which can see them and give them the accepting attention that they need in order to let go. As you become more familiar with your spells, it is startling to recognize that they have never been allowed to have their experience. You are so trained to turn away from them that they never felt heard. I assure you, the joy that comes when you truly recognize and listen to a part of yourself that you have denied, fallen into, or run away from your whole life is delicious.

It is also delicious to finally recognize that it is okay to be experiencing whatever you are experiencing. Discovering how to meet ourselves exactly as we are brings forth such joy. We have been waiting a long time to heal the spell that it is not okay to authentically be ourselves. It takes time to learn this because we have been conditioned to turn away from what we are experiencing rather than toward it. Patience is key in this kind of healing. It is like learning a new language: the language of the heart. Your heart carries an energy of healing that is beyond any fixing, changing, or resisting that your mind can do. Your heart is all about nonjudgment, inclusion, allowing, willingness to listen, and acceptance.

There is a wonderful thing you can do with your imagination to help you see what your spells are asking of you so that you can discover your own pathway from your reactive mind to your attentive heart. Imagine coming into a large room that seems to be empty. Suddenly a movement in the corner captures your attention. As you walk toward this corner, you see it is a frightened little child who is trying to hide. In a flash, you know this child is feeling exactly what you have been feeling. What would you say? How would you be with this child? Whatever response you have is exactly what your feelings want from you. Turn your attention toward yourself and be with yourself in the exact way you would be with this child.

If this pathway doesn't call to you, you can also imagine what you would have liked your parents to say to you and how you would have liked them to be with you. Or you can imagine your mate or your friends doing the same. Right here, in your imagination, is what you need from yourself.

156

There are two other wonderful practices you can add to your life, as well. First, whenever you find yourself caught in struggle, bring your hand to the area of your body that is tightening. If you are angry, you may feel something like a fist in your stomach. If you are sad, you could feel a lump in your throat. Gently lay your hand there, and as you bring your full attention to that area say, "I see you. It is okay that you are here." Remember, you are not trying to make anything happen. Just a moment or two of bringing your full attention to your immediate experience makes a difference in the long run.

Second, if it is not clear what is reacting inside of you, you can bring your hand to your heart and either pat or circle it around your chest and say, "I accept myself as I am." Remember, when you recognize that the meadow of your being *is* Love, you finally know that there is not a part of you that doesn't deserve to be included in the meadow. Then you realize that no matter what Life brings up inside of you, all is welcome here.

So the question is, how do you want to live? Do you want to live from your mind, lost in your clouds of struggle and listening to a storyteller that reacts and controls, or do you want to live from your heart, which opens you to Life? For most of us, that choice becomes very clear. We want to move beyond our addiction to struggle and meet ourselves and our lives with the healing of our hearts.

KEY POINTS

- To be fully open to Life, you need to be open to whatever is going on inside you.

- There is a whole host of characters within you that you don't want anybody else to know about. There is no need to be ashamed of these. Everybody has them.

- It is your heart that can approach these characters, listen to their views of the world, and thus release them from the prison of your resistance to them.

- Your mind is dualistic by nature; it likes/dislikes, wants/resists all day long. Your heart is the opposite, for it is a lover of what is. It includes rather than excludes. It accepts rather than rejects, and it can weave every single part of you back into the whole that it truly is.

- When you were young, your heart center was open. As you shut it down, you retreated into your mind and locked the innocence and healing power of your heart deep inside of you.

- When your heart begins to open again, you discover the healing power of not resisting what you are experiencing. This brings you to the phenomenal healing power of "All is welcome here."

- There is nobody to blame. Your parents (and siblings) were just the delivery system for the wounds you took on and that are here to teach you about your heart.

- Transformation happens in an atmosphere of acceptance and listening. When you give accepting attention, the tightly held energy that has been bound up inside begins to expand and move.

- You don't need to be fixed. Fixing is the endless game of the storyteller that comes from being taught to judge and fear what goes on inside of you.

- Most of your pain is your resistance to your pain.

- The spells that you have bought into throughout your life are not you. They are just conditioned states that keep you separate from the meadow of your being.

-

REMEMBERING   Week 7
This week's Remembering Statement:
All is welcome here.
Your own statement:

Remembering Session

Each week as you have worked with this book, you have been deepening your ability to bring your attention and your immediate experience together. It is now time to discover that you can relate directly to whatever you are experiencing rather than being lost in it or running away from it.

This week, as you are riding the waves of your breath, when your storyteller and the feelings and sensations that it generates grab your attention, you are invited to be curious about what has grabbed your attention. It may be a story about what happened yesterday or a pain in your arm or a feeling of sadness in your chest. Say, "I see you" to whatever you are noticing and then return to your breath. This allows you to relate to what you are experiencing rather than being identified with it.

"I see you" accesses the phenomenal healing of your heart. It is saying, "For this moment, I am giving my full, accepting attention to whatever I am noticing." You will have time in the next Remembering Session to actually explore what is taking you away. For now, see it, acknowledge it by saying "I see you," and then return to your breath and to the calming/focusing words. Remember, everything you notice is just an expression of the clouds of struggle, and the invitation is to acknowledge it, let it go, and come back to the sanctuary of your breath.

Some days you will easily see what has captured your attention and effortlessly return to the ground of your breath. Other days your storyteller will be very strong. Then, when you come back to your breath, your attention will immediately bounce back into its stories. It doesn't matter if your attention goes back into your storyteller and stays there. Even a single moment of relating to your experience by saying "I see you" matters.

This is why there is no such thing as a good session or a bad session. Some of the most powerful sessions you will have are when your storyteller is all stirred up and you have only moments when you recognize that your attention is again caught in your mind. With that recognition, you will more and more easily be able to let go of your stories.

After you read the following section, put down the book, close your eyes, and begin exploring. If you are timing your session, add one minute to the previous session for a total of eleven minutes. If time is not an issue, stay with each step as long as your curiosity is engaged.

Let's begin:

⁌ Close your eyes and check in, noticing what it is like to be you right now.

For at least three in-breaths, tighten your muscles, and then very slowly relax everything on your out-breath as you say the great sound of letting go, *Ahh!*

Bring your attention to the circle of your breath, saying the calming/focusing words, "In . . . out. Deep . . . slow. Calm . . . ease. As is . . . I'm here." (Or you can say "As is . . . I'm here" by itself.)

Whenever you notice that you are no longer fully with your breath, be curious about what your attention has been drawn to. Say to whatever you are noticing, "I see you" or "I see you; I'm here," if that resonates with you.

If you feel called to do so, spend some time using curiosity to explore what you are noticing. If not, simply bring your attention back to your breath and the calming/focusing words. Know that every moment of saying "I see you" and then returning to your breath is a moment of healing.

At the end, expand your awareness and be curious about your experience of giving yourself the healing of your own attention.

When you are ready, open your eyes. ⸭

Abbreviated Version

⸭ Close your eyes and check in, noticing what it is like to be you right now.

For at least three in-breaths, tighten your muscles, and then very slowly relax everything on your out-breath as you say the great sound of letting go, *Ahh!*

Bring your attention to the circle of your breath, saying the calming/focusing words.

Whenever you notice that you are no longer fully with your breath, be curious about what your attention has been drawn to.

Whatever you notice, say, "I see you," and then bring your attention back to your breath and the calming/focusing words.

At the end, expand your awareness and be curious about your experience after having given yourself the healing of your own attention.

When you are ready, open your eyes. ⸭

8

All Is Well—Come Here

You are on the journey back to the meadow of your being, discovering along the way how to be curious about *what is* rather than trying to control it. Learning how to turn toward your experience rather than away from it allows you access to the powerful healing force of your own heart. Through the heart, all of the energy that was tightly held by the spells you took on can now be released. The more bound-up energy you release, the more you show up for Life and the more you rediscover the meadow of your natural okayness, where everything flows, everything is alive, and everything is Love.

As you are gathering the insight and the willingness to be compassionately attentive to what you are experiencing rather than identifying with it, it is helpful to imagine that you come in three layers.

The top layer is your mind. Instead of using it to be curious about Life, you (like most people) have turned it into a storyteller that narrates your world. Your storyteller is based on fear and glued together by judgment, and it talks all day long. Its world is all about controlling you and controlling Life. It likes and dislikes, trying to get to what it wants and getting rid of what it doesn't. When it can't change you and your life in the way it wants, it will often turn to compulsions to numb you. It is this resistance to your immediate experience, and your identification with all the stories that come out of resistance, that creates the clouds that fill your head.

The second layer is made up of all of the so-called unacceptable, unmet parts of yourself. These are parts that you don't want yourself or anybody else to know about, so the controlling, compulsive top layer buries them deep inside you. They are the youngest, most vulnerable parts of you that are afraid they are not good enough, that they are too much of this and not enough of that, and that Life is not safe. These parts are so full of despair that you feel if you come close to them, you might drown. Although you keep them buried, they don't go away. Instead, they influence you from underneath your everyday awareness.

The bottom layer is who you really are. It is the meadow of your being. When you live from this place, there is a twinkle in your eye, an aliveness in your body, and a vibrancy and radiance in your being. In the meadow you are no longer caught up in *doing* Life. Instead you are *being* Life, reconnecting with your natural trust that allows you to show up for Life rather than being stuck in your head, always trying to make it be what you think it should be. This is the place you lived when you were very young, until many of the feelings and sensations you were experiencing became too much and you buried them inside (second layer) and retreated to your head (top layer).

On this journey back to yourself, the meadow is the place that opens up when you discover how to use your mind (the top layer) to be curious about what you are experiencing. The meadow reveals itself when you are interested in—rather than endlessly trying to fix, understand, and generally resist—what is going on inside of you, especially the most hidden and unacceptable parts (the second layer). Through the power of curiosity, you can cut through the storyteller's penchant for resisting your experience, and you can bring to the top layer the nonjudgmental awareness that allows it to relax. To the second layer you can offer the accepting attention it needs in order to move through you at last. The more you meet your immediate experience with an aware heart, the more you discover an amazing truth: every single part of you that you resisted because you were afraid or ashamed of it contains a doorway back into the joy and peace of the meadow (the bottom layer).

❦ Take a moment now, and dip the finger of your attention
into the river of your experience. The meadow is right
here with you. Don't try to find it; just use your mind to
notice Life. Fully experience Life, right here, right now. ❧

The most important truth is that right now, as you are reading this
book, you are the meadow. Your body is filled with radiance, your
heart is full of love, and in every cell of your being there is deep trust
in the flow of Life. All of these generate a spaciousness within you
that rests in the vast stillness at the heart of Life.

And yet most of the time you don't notice this meadow of your
being. Instead, you pay attention to the clouds in your head, which are
made up of all sorts of spells you took on when you were young. The
storyteller, the voice of the clouds, talks all day as it tries to manage
Life. It doesn't know how to engage with Life right here, right now.

You are being invited to move beyond management of Life and into
engagement with Life. This is what you long for: the joy of opening to
Life and trusting it. Remember that trust is not trusting that you will
get what you want. Trust understands that you will get what you *need*
in order to come out of the clouds of struggle. Trust trusts both the
easy and the difficult aspects of Life.

There is a wonderful quote from Erich Fromm, philosopher, psycho-
analyst, and author of *The Art of Loving*, that speaks directly to the sense
of trust needed in order to show up for Life: "If one does not know that
everything has its time, and wants to force things, then indeed one will
never succeed in becoming concentrated—nor in the art of loving."

As you soften into the flow of Life, knowing, as it says in the Bible
"to everything there is a season," then you become what Fromm calls
"concentrated." This means showing up for what is here—both the
easy and the difficult—and discovering that there are no ordinary
moments in your life. Life is speaking to you at all times, showing
you the spells you took on. Fromm's quote brings it all together in the
statement about the art of loving. He understood that as you learn to
see your spells with love, your clouds of struggle thin, and you discover that this whole journey is about becoming Love.

So you are getting to know your storyteller—not to fix it, change it, or get rid of it, but to see it for what it is: a storyteller that is based on fear and judgment, created in your mind when you were a child. The more you can see it, the more your clouds can dissipate, and the more you can know and live from the meadow of your being again.

FOUR TOOLS OF AWAKENING

We have explored four tools for transforming your storyteller:

- partnering with the Intelligence of Life
- cultivating curiosity
- changing your relationship with discomfort
- accessing the power of your heart

The following is an overview of these four powerful tools. When you are caught in struggle, they can quickly remind you how to recognize and unhook from your clouds.

Partnering with the Intelligence of Life

Asking for clarity from Life comes from knowing that you are not alone. The Intelligence of Life is with you every step of the way. The more you access this Intelligence, the more you discover you are not the one in charge of your healing. Thinking that you are is like a peach tree thinking it needs to create its peaches—and feeling it is not doing so well enough or fast enough. Life is in charge of Life, and just as the forces of Life are working together to bring forth a peach, they are working together in your life to bring you into consciousness.

You can access the Intelligence of Life by asking questions without looking for an answer. This can be frustrating in the beginning because you are so used to trying to find an answer. But seeking answers accesses only your mind, which has a limited capacity to understand what is truly going on. Asking questions of Life bypasses your struggling mind and is one of the most powerful tools you are given by Life.

You can ask questions of Life as you move throughout your day. The one I use the most is "In this situation, what do I need to say, do, or be that is for the highest good?" It still delights me to see the depth of wisdom that moves through me when I turn a challenge over to Life. I say and do things I couldn't even comprehend the moment before I asked Life for clarity.

Questions can be helpful in taking you right to what you are experiencing. Here is an example from a woman named Lucille in one of my phone groups:

> It's been a pretty stressful, anxious time lately. Yesterday I stopped by the grocery store after work to pick up a couple things for dinner. I saw a little display touting this black, Finnish licorice, and all of a sudden I *had* to have licorice. After some debate, I put it in my basket, and while I was waiting in the checkout line, I was thinking about how I could eat it in the car, how good it would taste, and how nobody would know that I'd had it.
>
> Finally I noticed that my stomach was getting tighter and tighter, but I still wanted licorice. By the time I got to the car, I was noticing my stomach more and the licorice a bit less. As I sat down behind the wheel, I put both my hands on my belly and asked, "What is asking to be seen inside of me?" My attention immediately settled into the tightness in my stomach, and I said to it, "I see you. I don't know what you're trying to tell me, but I see you, and I'll try to listen." Suddenly I didn't need to eat the licorice, and it wasn't even particularly interesting anymore. I drove home, made dinner, and ate it with my family—all without licorice.

Lucille's willingness to ask Life for clarity in seeing what was going on inside of her lessened the grip of the spells she was experiencing and also woke up her curiosity. As it became interesting to bring her attention to the tightness in her stomach, her heart woke up and began to give the tightness the compassionate acceptance it was longing for. Through being seen, the urge to numb herself with licorice became less interesting than being with herself. And all of this happened from the willingness to ask a question.

It is amazing how most people faced with a challenge totally forget that the Intelligence of Life is always with them, waiting to be of assistance. Examples of questions to ask are "What is asking to be met here?" or "What am I ready to see?" or "What is the way through this?" You can ask these when what is arising within you is too big to unhook from and you are caught in resistance, when it is unclear exactly what is going on, or when Life is moving too fast for you to take the time to turn your attention within and see what is going on.

The power of these questions is in the questions themselves. They signal Life that you are ready to listen to wisdom that comes from beyond your mind and that you are ready to see what you formerly resisted. Remember, whenever you ask this kind of question, you set events in motion. When you first tap into the power of asking questions without looking for an answer, your mind will look for answers, doubt that they will come, and may even give up easily saying, "This doesn't work." But it does work, and answers will come to you—in Life's time and in Life's way.

⁜ Ask Life what it is that you are ready to see inside of you and then let that question work its magic from underneath your everyday awareness. ⁜

Cultivating Curiosity

Everything we have explored comes under the umbrella of being curious in an accepting way about what you are experiencing. This ability to turn toward your experience rather than getting lost in it or denying it is one of the most powerful awakening tools available to a human being. Curiosity is powerful because you step out of your storyteller's point of view. Now you are relating *to* it rather than *from* it. You don't need to understand exactly what is going on. The simple recognition that you are caught opens a space around your contraction, allowing you to see it from a broader perspective.

As your curiosity develops, you will be fascinated with what is going on inside of you, especially when you are triggered by Life. At those times, you will be able to say, "I am going to let what is happening inside of me take place." You will be able to fully experience whatever you are experiencing without getting distracted by what your storyteller says about it. As you give your experience the fullness of your accepting attention, you can often feel the energy that was bound up inside of you beginning to move and let go.

As you see what your storyteller is up to, you will discover how to accept your experience of even the scary, dark, and so-called negative parts of yourself. These are not "bad" parts that need to be eliminated. You are a mixture of dark and light, just like the yin-yang symbol reminds us. Your dark parts are full of richness and gifts, which they will reveal to you when they receive the light of your accepting attention.

Thich Nhat Hanh, the beloved Buddhist monk and author, discusses this in the book *Thich Nhat Hanh: The Joy of Full Consciousness* when he writes, "The fear, anger, and suffering in us are like useful compost. We must not try to throw them out the window. They are quite necessary in order for flowers like compassion, joy, and happiness to bloom in us. . . . [This] is the basis of all our practice. Without it, we will continue to suffer. We will continue to believe that we have to get rid of these negative states in order to be happy. On the contrary, it is very important to accept them."

A woman named Clara, who attended one of my groups, shared her insights about accepting her darker moods and acknowledging that they were temporary:

> I was cooking dinner and looking around at my messy house, and the thought/spell came into my mind: "I'm tired and overwhelmed." Once I bought into that story, I noticed my energy sink. Then my perception shifted, and I realized that *the tired and overwhelmed parts of me are here.* That small shift didn't cause the same energy sink; instead it created more spaciousness. I then said, "The tired and overwhelmed ones are visiting." What a shift that made! It acknowledge that it's all temporary, that this too shall pass. It opened me even more spaciousness.

I then had some insights about the meadow/clouds analogy. The stories in our minds are just like the weather—it comes and goes. Some days it's sunny, some days it's rainy, some days it's snowy, etc. I can't control the weather, and it's not permanent. It's always shifting and impossible to control. The only choice is to experience it as it is—to see it.

Through turning toward her experience, Clara did not fall into identification with her storyteller, so she could be with what she was experiencing rather than being lost in it. Also, Clara's energy of tiredness didn't get trapped inside because she didn't resist it. Instead, it simply passed through like the weather passes through the sky.

When allowing your stories to pass through you, it is helpful to soften your belly and breathe into the experience, for it is in softening around your stories that they let go. It is truly a delight when you discover how often you hold your breath when a spell has taken over and how powerful it is to allow the energy of your breath to flow. A deep, full breath moves energy. Rather than trying to take a deep breath, which can bring more tension because you are *trying* to breathe deeply, focus on your out-breath. For as many breaths as you are called to take, let them be long, slow, and deep. Focusing on your out-breath calms your mind and brings an opening around what is trying to close. (You can access a long, slow out-breath through the candle breath exercise in the Remembering Session for Week 2.)

> ❦ Bring your attention to your belly. If it's tight,
> recognize your storyteller is holding on. Do the candle
> breath to access some long, deep out-breaths. Then allow
> a smile to go all the way down into your belly. ❧

Changing Your Relationship with Discomfort

In order to know and live from the spaciousness of the meadow, it is important to change your relationship with discomfort. Rather than resisting it, you go toward it. You move beyond wanting to hold it at bay or falling into it. When you move toward discomfort, whatever is happening becomes workable rather than taking you over. When you realize the healing that comes from being with an experience you formerly ran away from, you become a tightness detective. Whenever your mind, body, or heart is tight, you become interested in what you are experiencing rather than being caught in resistance. Remember, anything that makes you tight is of the fight (of the clouds of struggle).

The more you awaken from your clouds, the more you realize there is nothing worth closing around. Rather than tightening around your discomfort, you finally see that you do not want all of your conditioned stories to be fueled by your identification with them. Nor do you want them stuffed back inside of you, where they can create all sorts of havoc. So you finally discover that the only choice is to experience what you are experiencing *as it is* and to give it your accepting attention. Then the bound-up energy has the space to move through you. Immeasurable joy results from recognizing a familiar story of struggle for what it is, just a conditioned story, instead of following it down the rabbit hole. And in that recognition lies the possibility of the spell's bound-up energy opening so it can be free to move through you rather than being stuffed down inside of you again.

Yes, many deeply hidden parts are painful when they come close to the surface, and it is the most uncomfortable states that need you the most. Once, when I was talking about the power of saying "I see you," a woman in one of my groups reported that she heard it as "ICU," the abbreviation for a hospital's "intensive care unit." She started laughing at the irony of that because she recognized that the parts of her that most needed to hear "I see you" are the ones that have been in survival mode the longest and thus are in the ICU. These parts desperately need to be heard. They need you to respond to your experience with as much curiosity and compassion as you can muster.

When you meet your deepest holdings, turning toward your experience can be like putting frozen fingers into warm water. As the blood flows back into your fingers, it hurts like hell. At times, when your attention touches and opens the bound-up parts of yourself, it can hurt as energy begins to flow again in your body and heart. But this is the hurt of healing. Just as your fingers feel alive again after warm blood returns, you feel much more alive when energy begins to flow through the bound-up parts of you.

If a very painful part is asking for your attention, it helps to breathe into the experience, opening it up from the inside with the gentle caress of your breath. It also helps to remember that nothing lasts. Every thought, feeling, and sensation you ever had eventually moved through you. They will all pass through much more quickly when met by your heart. Remember, this is just bound-up energy that wants to move rather than remaining caught in the web of your resistance. Know that your heart is up to the task of opening that constricted energy.

Dora, a woman I have worked with for a while, shared her story of the joy of meeting even the deepest of spells inside of us.

⸙ As you read the following story, check in with your breath and notice if it is holding. If so, allow yourself one long *Ahh* out-breath. ⸙

I went into a contracted place after a friend's death. The contrast to the openness and expansion I had been feeling was painful, and I was struggling. I turned my attention inside and asked who was there, and a terrified one showed up. It was a new feeling—an intense feeling of terror—and it was connected to dying. I realized my mind was terrified of dying, and my friend's death allowed me to see this part. I didn't even know it was here to that degree. I couldn't see or feel it before because I had pushed it away so thoroughly. But the terror had been simmering underneath my everyday awareness for a very long time.

Even though I had been working with the scared one—welcoming it and feeling pretty good about it—on this occasion my mind was screaming. This part felt like being trapped in a small room trying to escape by frantically banging against the walls. It ᶠ ¹·¹ ' to breathe, but rather than running away, I just noticed it.

᷾f the feelings without trying to change anything.

ed to the scared one: "Of course, sweetie—of course d be here. You see death as the end, so why wouldn't you be terrified? Let's get to know each other. I'm sorry I haven't really seen you before this. You're beautiful. All is welcome here. You are welcome here. You are well—come here."

I felt such tenderness for this part of me in that moment. I held it in my heart and let it be. I even told it that it could stay as long as it needed to—and I meant it. It was an incredible experience.

I'm excited to get to know my terrified one better and to develop a relationship with it. I've sat with it every morning, connecting, saying hello. Such a gift! Such a gift!

❄ Notice what Dora's willingness to explore terror brought up inside of you. Then give whatever you are experiencing the gift of a smile. ❄

Dora could say "such a gift!" because the hidden terror that influenced her from beneath her everyday awareness her whole life was finally seen and enfolded in her heart. Also, the energy that was bound up in the terror and in her resistance to it was freed up, bringing her back to the joy and the spaciousness of the meadow of her being. She trusted Life enough to open up to this terror so it could let go, which brings us back to the core message of this book: *Life is set up to bring up what has been bound up, so it can open up to be freed up, so you can show up for Life.*

Accessing the Power of Your Heart

Spells that don't let go under the light of your attention are asking for the healing of your heart. It is through your heart that you can finally see how scared, angry, lost, and lonely your storyteller is. The more you learn how to be curious and ask Life for clarity, the more your heart will naturally open. When the formerly unacceptable parts of yourself—all is welcome here—are met with your aware heart, then lasting healing occurs.

It is your heart that knows how to embrace rather than resist your experience. Remember, we accessed the powerful heal of the heart in the last chapter through the phrases "All is w here," "As is . . . I'm here," and "I see you . . . I'm here." The

the place where you move beyond fighting with what is and instead give it the space that it needs to move through you. It is the heart that naturally knows the acceptance, spaciousness, and listening that every single part of you is longing for.

Rhonda, a participant in one of my Awakening Groups, was willing to ask questions and meet her fears with a healing heart. Her story vividly illustrates the type of dialogue you can have with your storyteller and the fearful parts of yourself.

⸙ As you read this story, put your hand over your heart to remind yourself to meet with accepting attention whatever arises within you. ⸙

I live with my grandmother, who is eighty-six, and she usually awakens by nine-thirty in the morning. I've never seen her get up later than ten-thirty in the six months I've been her caretaker. In the quiet of the morning, as time slowly approached the ten-thirty mark, my storyteller began to weave its tale: "She never sleeps this late. It's strange that she isn't up yet, don't you think?" Rather than hooking into its story, I took a deep breath, placed my hand over my heart, and said "hello" to this fear-based story, reminding it that it was welcome here.

This time the storyteller didn't want to be interrupted, so it continued to tell an even more entrancing story: "It's unusually quiet. I can't hear her snoring. And I usually hear her get up and use the bathroom in the night, and I didn't. She has died in her sleep. She's dead! My grandmother is dead. I know it. I can feel it! I don't want to lose her, and now I won't have a place to live, so what am I going to do?" I could feel myself getting drawn back into my stories of fear.

Heart pounding, neck and shoulders tensed, arms closed across a tight belly, I felt my curiosity wake up and coax me out of reaction. "This is just the storyteller," it said. My shoulders dropped slightly, and I invited my neck to relax. With one hand on my heart and another on my softening belly, I said, "Who's here?" Immediately it was clear that it was the scared one. "Oh, sweetheart," I said, "it's okay that you're here. We're safe. Life is in charge, and all is well."

As my belly softened, my shoulders relaxed, and I opened into the spaciousness of touching my fear with my heart. Then the stories arose again. For forty-five minutes this dance continued. The lyrics from the storyteller increased in detail, but I was anchored by my breath's rhythm and my willingness to be compassionately curious about what the storyteller was doing.

Tightness would overtake me but then I would soften around it. It was like watching a wave hit the shore and then recede. I was not the wave with its troughs and peaks; I was the witness of the wave in all its beauty and glory, and it was breathtaking and magnificent to watch.

As it approached eleven o'clock, the time I had decided to check on my grandmother, the storyteller was building more elaborate plots. First I closed around fear, but then my heart would accept it, allow it, and not need to change it. Then I watched the fear build again, and again my heart enveloped it with love. With every wave, the heart deepened until the storyteller was completely enveloped in love.

As I opened my grandmother's door, I heard her deep breathing and then the loud ring from the phone on her nightstand. As she jumped up to answer the phone, I shut the door, smiling at the truly rich gift she had given me by sleeping in. Then my storyteller said, "Oh, I'm so stupid! I thought she was dead. I made such a big deal out of nothing." And my heart responded, "Oh, sweetheart, I love you just as you are!" The dance continued.

When Rhonda shared her experience with me, I asked her to write it down so I could include it in the book. At the end of it she wrote, "A whole cast of characters has shown up in this experience, and, amazingly, I have welcomed each one into my heart with love and open arms. And you know, not one stayed very long! Even with the one inside of me that believed that I wouldn't be able to write down this experience in the right way (and thus, I am doing life wrong), I could lovingly remind her that Life is doing Life, and it is safe."

Rhonda concluded, "To let it all go and to trust this process, to not be caught in any of the stories that were trying to catch me yesterday, to have the openness and love in my heart to allow them to pass through me, and to continue to return over and over to my truth that Life is for us—and it is trustable—what a game changer and peace bringer. I am so filled with gratitude!"

In spite of being caught in a deep spell of fear, Rhonda was able to realize that it was just her storyteller, and she gave it the compassionate attention it needed. Even when you recognize the powerful healing that comes when you can meet your experience with your heart, there will still be times when your heart won't open. Remember that noticing you are caught in your storyteller and turning the situation over to Life are enough. These are the foundational tools of awakening. And the more you turn toward yourself, the more your heart will effortlessly open.

It is very important not to force the opening of your heart. Now that you know how powerful it is to touch your experience with your heart, your mind will try to "do" the opening of your heart and will get frustrated when meeting your experience doesn't do what you want it to do. ("I am saying 'I see you,' and nothing is happening," says the mind.) But it doesn't work to give your accepting attention to something in hopes that it will let go. The bound-up parts inside of you are very sensitive to subtle feelings of wanting them to go away. True "letting go" happens when all the parts are fully seen, fully accepted, and, if needed, fully heard *without* you needing them to be any different than they are.

One of the biggest moments in the healing of my own fear came when, with deep sincerity, I said to the scared one inside of me, "If you need to be here for my whole life, that is okay." Looking back at that time, I can see now that my fear calmed down dramatically after it was met in that way.

So you are not trying to make something happen. Instead of trying to fix it, you are using your mind in a new way: to bring enough curiosity to your experience so that your heart can naturally open. This is about purely relating to your experience. Those moments of true relating culminate in a shift of perception that brings healing beyond anything you can even imagine right now. Under the gaze of accepting attention, the energy that was bound up inside of you is transformed back into the free-flowing aliveness it came from.

❧ Turn your attention to yourself and be curious about what you are experiencing right now. Allow your experience to develop like a Polaroid picture. Whatever you notice—a feeling, a sensation, or a story—say to it, "I see you." ❧

A GRADUAL AWAKENING

Know that each moment of curiosity and each moment of compassion matters. Every time you meet your experience, it is like a drop of water is added to a bucket that is sitting at your feet. After a few times of turning toward your experience, you look down, and there are a couple of drops of water in the bucket. So your mind says, "This is not working." But as you continue to be drawn to being compassionately curious, one day you'll look down and the bucket is half full, and every drop of water represents a moment of curiosity. Even so, the mind will say this is not enough. But one day, with unexplainable joy, you will discover that your feet are wet. The bucket is overflowing.

In this journey of discovering how to bring your accepting attention to whatever you are experiencing, one day you may notice you're caught, but you may forget to turn it over to Life. Another day you may come across something that is so deep and disturbing to your mind that you can barely recognize that you are caught, and you won't know what to do except turn it over to Life. Other days you can easily notice the lump in your throat, and it lets go just by being seen. Then there will be times when you can recognize the tightness in your neck, but you won't have a clue what it is telling you.

As you move deeper into awakening, there will be times that you easily see and hear core spells, releasing the energy that was formerly bound up in them. Your whole body will then glow with the energy that has been opened. It is important to know that whatever opens up for you, you can be with yourself for just seconds, or you can spend half an hour exploring your immediate experience. Trust what is calling to you.

Also, there will be times you don't want to turn toward your experience. When you are caught in the reactions of your spells, you may want to get rid of them, get lost in them, or blame others for causing them. The question I ask you is, "Has this ever brought you the peace you long for?" In the short run, it may bring you the feeling of getting away from what you don't want to look at, and it may also give you the illusion of control. In the long run, however, it just keeps you caught in your clouds, cutting you off from the meadow of your being.

As you become willing to be curious and give your immediate experience accepting attention, you discover an amazing thing: healing doesn't come from fixing, changing, or getting rid of anything. It doesn't even come from letting go of anything. It comes when these formerly bound-up parts receive full acceptance, and *they* let go. This is what Rumi is saying in the last half of his poem "The Guest House":

> Welcome difficulty.
> Learn the alchemy True Human
> Beings know:
> the moment you accept what troubles
> you've been given, a door opens.

Rumi is not talking about intellectual acceptance. Accepting difficulties and the challenges in your life is an essential part of your journey, and in this acceptance, you can then explore them. And in that exploration, a door opens.

So in this process of discovering the doorways to the parts of yourself that you have tried the most to stay away from, please remember that awakening isn't something you do; it is something you discover that you are. Your natural state is curiosity, and all we are doing here is waking it up so it can dispel the clouds of your conditioning.

KEY POINTS

- Rather than trying to fix, get rid of, or understand what you are experiencing, the most powerful way to open bound-up energy is with your attention, for when your attention and your immediate experience come together, bound-up energy begins to move.

- By learning how to turn toward your experience rather than away from it, you access the powerful healing force of your own heart. The energy that was tightly held in all the spells you took on can now let go, and the more they let go, the more you naturally rediscover the meadow of your being.

- You are not alone. The Intelligence of Life has been with you every step of the way. The more you access it, you also discover you are not the one in charge of your healing.

- The heart is the place where you move beyond fighting with what is and instead give it the space that it needs to move through.

- Become a tightness detective, because what makes you tight is the fight (of the clouds of struggle). Go toward discomfort. Then everything becomes workable rather than overwhelming.

- The more you awaken out of the clouds of your conditioning, the more you realize there is nothing worth closing around.

- You don't want your conditioned stories to be fueled by your identification with them, nor do you want them stuffed back inside of you, where they can create all sorts of havoc.

- As your attention begins to touch and open the bound-up parts of yourself, it can hurt. But this is the hurt of healing.

- Applying the healing power of your heart isn't about trying to make something happen. It is about moments of purely relating with your experience. And these moments of pure relating bring healing beyond anything you can even imagine right now.

- Healing doesn't come from fixing, changing, getting rid of, or even letting go of anything. It comes when these formerly bound-up parts receive full acceptance, and they let go.

-

-

-

REMEMBERING   Week 8
This week's Remembering Statement:
What does this bring up in me?
Your own statement:

Remembering Session

You may have discovered in previous sessions that there were certain experiences—stories in your head, sensations in your body, or deep feelings—that didn't quiet down when you said to them, "I see you." The parts of you that keep grabbing your attention are just trapped energy, and they are asking you to listen to them so they can let go.

When you encounter these parts, it is the time to create a relationship with whatever you are experiencing, and you do that by saying, "Tell me about your world." Remember, all of these parts of you are just like you. Whether it is a busy mind that wants to plan the rest of the day, an ache in your stomach, a lump of tears in your throat, or a feeling of anxiousness in your chest, each of these parts has a particular view of the world—a view that was most likely formed and frozen inside you when you were young. Just like you, your various parts calm down when they are heard. When you can bring your aware heart to your experience, giving these parts the kind of listening they need to let go, your clouds of struggle thin, and the meadow is more available to you.

It is important to remember that you are not trying to make anything happen. The parts of you that are longing to be heard are very sensitive to your slightest desire to make them go away. You are not trying to let go of anything or make anything let go. That comes from the old paradigm that believes that if you fix, change, or get rid of whatever is arising inside of you, then you will know peace. This doesn't work. In fact, it actually energizes what you are trying to get beyond. You are simply interested in listening, in a compassionate way, to what draws you away from your breath. And in that listening, the bound-up energy in that feeling/thought/sensation is given the space to move and let go when it is ready.

After you read the following section, put down your book, close your eyes, and begin exploring. If you are timing your session, add one minute to the previous session for a total of twelve minutes. If time is not an issue, stay with each step as long as your curiosity is engaged.

Let's begin:

⊰ Close your eyes and dip the finger of your attention into the river of your experience, noticing what it is like to be you right now.

For three in-breaths, tighten your muscles, and then very slowly relax everything on your out-breath as you say the great sound of letting go, *Ahh!*

Bring your attention to the circle of your breath, saying
the calming/focusing words, "In . . . out. Deep . . . slow.
Calm . . . ease. As is . . . I'm here." (Or say "As is . . . I'm
here" by itself.)

When you notice your attention has drifted away from
the circle of your breath and the calming/focusing
words, ask yourself, "What is asking to be seen?" This
question is about turning your attention toward
yourself in this very moment and looking clearly into
your own experience.

If you notice a feeling/sensation/story, explore it with your
accepting attention. Say to whatever you are noticing, "I
see you. It is okay that you are here. I want to know about
your world." Remember, every single part of us has a view
of the world, a view that was formed before we were six.
And these parts respond to being heard just like you do.
So these words are inviting you to be fully with whatever
is there without falling into it, giving it the healing of
your own heart.

Whatever story/feeling/sensation you are exploring may
be ready to share with you its view of the world. Don't
force this. Let it come naturally. If nothing happens, know
that it has heard your willingness to hear about its world
and will share it with you when it is ready.

Stay with this curiosity for as long as it interests you,
from a few seconds to a few minutes. If you find yourself
getting fuzzy, let go of the exploration and come back to
the circle of your breath.

If you can't see clearly what is taking you away, know
that asking, "What is asking to be seen?" will set things

in motion. Then simply bring your attention back to the circle of your breath.

At the end, expand your awareness and be curious about your experience after having given yourself the healing of your own attention.

When you are ready, open your eyes. ⸙

Abbreviated Version

⸙ Close your eyes and check in, noticing what it is like to be you right now.

For three in-breaths, tighten your muscles, and then very slowly relax everything on your out-breath as you say the great sound of letting go, *Ahh!*

Bring your attention to the circle of your breath, saying the calming/focusing words, "In . . . out. Deep . . . slow. Calm . . . ease. As is . . . I'm here." (Or say "As is . . . I'm here" by itself.)

When you notice your attention has drifted away from the circle of your breath and the calming/focusing words, ask yourself, "What is asking to be seen?"

If you notice something, explore it with your accepting attention and say to it, "I see you. It is okay that you are here. I want to know about your world."

Stay with this curiosity for as long as it interests you. If you find yourself getting fuzzy, let the exploration go and come back to the circle of your breath.

At the end, expand your awareness and be curious about your experience after having given yourself the healing of your own attention.

When you are ready, open your eyes. ✻

9

Life Is *for* You

Throughout this book we have been exploring a radical shift of perception: the healing you long for doesn't come from changing anything. It comes from the ability to see and be with what is, for who you are is awareness. As awareness you can see, without wanting them to be any different than what they are, the spells, feelings, and sensations that pass through you all day long rather than being lost in the stories your storyteller generates about them.

When you learn how to be curious about what is going on inside of you, you discover the ability to experience what you are experiencing without turning it into a problem. You can then give the energy that was bound up in your struggles the attention and the spaciousness it needs in order to let go. This brings you back to the free-flowing aliveness that you truly are—the meadow of your being.

In order to be this curious about what is going on rather than always trying to control it, it is important to know that your life is *for* you. Life is not just a random series of events that happen because you did it right or you did it wrong. Instead, it is an intelligent unfolding that is revealing itself to you all day long, bringing you step by step from unconsciousness to consciousness. Or, as Eckhart Tolle says in his book *A New Earth,* "Life will give you whatever experience is most helpful for the evolution of your consciousness. How do you know this is the experience you need? Because this is the experience you are having at the moment."

Take a moment now to feel how different that is from the way you usually perceive Life: as something happening to you that needs to be controlled, fixed, and changed. Imagine what it would be like to let go of the whole game of resisting Life and instead to trust it. In this trust, you could then open to Life, listen to it, and grow from every encounter.

At a retreat I led on the Hawaiian island of Molokai, the core focus was "All is welcome here." On the second day, one of the participants said that whenever that phrase was spoken, she heard "All is well. Come here!" When you learn how to stop trying to make your life be what you want it to be and show up for it instead ("All is welcome here"), you discover that all is well (the meadow is always with you, and Life knows what it is doing), and it is safe to come here. You can show up for the life that Life is giving you. When neurosurgeon Eben Alexander, author of *Proof of Heaven*, woke up from his seven-day coma, the first thing he said to his sister was, "All is well!"

In order to open to "All is well," it is important to recognize that the evolution that is unfolding on Earth includes human beings. Everything is a part of this evolution, including you. You are Life evolving from unconsciousness to consciousness. Your life is not a random series of events. It is an intelligent and mysterious process that is *for* Life.

I like to call this unfolding the flawless, methodical mystery. It is flawless because each and every experience of your life is tailor-made to wake you out of your unconsciousness. Also, the unfolding is truly methodical. There are basic steps we all go through on our journey out of the clouds in our minds and back into recognition of the meadow of our being. And it is truly mysterious. Without fully understanding it, we can open to it, rediscovering what Joseph Campbell describes as "the rapture of being alive."

THE SIX PHASES OF CONSCIOUSNESS
Your life is a journey from unconsciousness to consciousness. Michael Bernard Beckwith, founder and spiritual director of the Agape

International Spiritual Center, describes this evolution in four phases. I have added two more, "Life happens in you" and "Life happens for you," and call them the six phases of consciousness.

- Life happens to you.
- Life happens by you.
- Life happens in you.
- Life happens for you.
- Life happens through you.
- Life is you.

Let us take a few minutes to explore each one. As you read, I invite you to keep on checking in with yourself. You are being given important information in this chapter. Remember that the most powerful thing you can do for your healing is to bring together your attention and your experience, even as you are reading this book and no matter what the information brings up for you.

> ❋ Dip the finger of your attention into the river of your experience. Allow whatever is here to be here. You have never experienced Life quite like this and never will again. This moment in your life is unique, and it is okay exactly as it is. ❧

Life Happens to You

For a good deal of your life you have probably lived like most human beings, feeling that Life is happening *to* you. Life is so big, and if you are honest with yourself, you never really know what is going to happen next. You wake up one morning, and your heart is light and happy, but the next day you're unsettled. Bosses fire you, the flu debilitates you, people you love reject you, every day you get a little older, and death is always lurking around the corner.

It is understandable that the more unconscious you are, the more often you feel like a victim of Life. When you live in the belief that Life is happening to you, you often view Life as a possible threat. So you stay caught in your head, finding yourself lost in your clouds of struggle and listening to a storyteller that resists, reacts, defends and explains, hoping to figure everything out. It generally does absolutely anything except be open to Life, right here, right now.

Life Happens by You

When it becomes too uncomfortable to live with this much powerlessness, you evolve into the belief that Life is happening *by* you. Rather than being a victim to Life, you believe you can control it. There can be a great feeling of personal power in this level of consciousness. It is a necessary step in moving out of the victimhood of the first phase, but people get caught there. Men try to control women and vice versa. Religions try to control the masses. Countries try to control other countries. The majority of people try to control others who are not like them—those who are gay, have a different skin color, or who follow dissimilar religions, for example. Most of all, we try to control ourselves, hoping to make ourselves be what we think we should be.

There is an enormous amount of effort in this level of consciousness. The storyteller believes that in order for anything good to happen, it has to make it happen. So it loves to set goals and feels very ashamed when it doesn't follow through (just think of New Year's resolutions). The storyteller eventually evolves into intentions. Goals are where you use your mind to try to make things be the way you want them. With intentions, you work with feeling what you want to generate. None of this is bad or wrong. These are important tools to use on the path of awakening, and sometimes they actually work. But what would happen if you recognized that rather than trying to make things happen, simply opening into Life will bring you what you most deeply long for?

There is a popular school of thought that teaches that you can control your reality. When you subscribe to this belief, the storyteller says that if you think the right thoughts, you can make your life be the way you want it. The main difficulty with this is that, in the long run, it doesn't work. To think you can control Life is like being a cork in the ocean believing it can direct the movement of the ocean. Yes, the cork's belief may change the movement of the water right where it is, but it can't influence all the other powerful forces that make up the ocean.

To stay caught in this phase of consciousness is to be cut off from the creative flow of Life. Believing that you are in charge of Life, you are mainly identified with your conceptual world, trying to create a reality rather than showing up for Reality.

When you have lived in this phase of consciousness long enough, you see the downside of it. First, you find yourself becoming fearful of your thoughts: "I shouldn't be thinking this way because I will manifest this in my world." Second, it can also bring forth shame, for when this belief doesn't work the way the self-help books promise, you think this is because you haven't done it right or well enough. Author and speaker Caroline Myss used to have a thread in her teachings that said you could manifest what you want if you just think right. By the time she gave a talk in Seattle in the 1990s, she had evolved beyond this phase. A friend who went to her talk told me that Myss asked the audience of six hundred to raise their hands if they had been able to create the reality they wanted. Not one person did.

> ⨯ As you are reading about Life happening *to* you
> and *by* you, your belly may have tightened. Allow any
> holding you discover there to melt away. Smile and let
> this softening move all the way down into your pelvic
> floor and around to your back. ⨯

Life Happens in You

You eventually begin to see that all of your reacting and controlling hasn't brought you the ease and joy you long for. Instead of being the victim or needing to make your life be any particular way, which is the endless game of struggle, you begin to get an inkling that Life is something to be listened to, opened to. This is where you start evolving into the next phase of consciousness: Life is happening *in* you.

At this level of consciousness you begin to realize something startling: rather than experiencing Life, most of the time you think about it, seeing only the thoughts in your head. When you experience Life through your thoughts, you stop experiencing it as it is. Or as the well-known French author Anaïs Nin said in her 1961 work *Seduction of the Minotaur*, "We don't see things as they are. We see them as we are." You project your spells onto yourself and others rather than really seeing what is. When was the last time you truly saw a loved one's face? If you are honest with yourself, it has probably been a long time.

It is in this phase that you also realize that your suffering doesn't come from the experiences of your life. Instead it comes from your stories about what is happening. It comes from inside of you. There could be a gray day, and you're just fine. Then on another gray day, you could be miserable. You may say it is because the day is gray, but it comes from your story about the day, not the day itself.

This is where you begin to live what we have been calling the "you-turn." You become less interested in being a victim of your life or even trying to make it be any different than it is. You realize that the healing you long for comes when you turn your attention within. When you get to know the spells that are the source of your suffering, you can unhook from them and come back to Life.

❧ Do a you-turn and ask, "What is asking to be seen?"
Be curious about what sits here right now. ☙

Life Happens for You

The more you become curious about what is happening rather than reacting and controlling, the more you come to a wonderful realization that your life is *for* you. Life is not a random series of events. It is a highly intelligent unfolding that is putting you in the exact situations you need in order to see and unhook from the spells that keep you separate from its flow. No matter what is happening in your life, you finally understand that Life knows what it is doing.

Rather than Life being something you have to mold and shape into what you want it to be, you begin to show up for Life exactly as it is. Yes, the flow of Life includes pain, loss, and death. But resisting the pains of Life only turn them into suffering, and the suffering that comes from resistance is always much greater than directly experiencing your pain. Instead of tightening around your experiences and turning away from them, which only thickens your clouds of struggle, you bring your attention to your experience, whatever it is.

Even little moments of curiosity sprinkled throughout your day are powerful. Every time you respond rather than react to what is going on inside of you, what was formerly bound up begins to loosen. Remember, your natural state is free-flowing aliveness. When that aliveness gets trapped in the spells, your energy and joy dim. When the spells receive the light of your attentiveness, they let go, and the trapped energy flows freely, bringing with it the bliss of openness. Remember, Life is set up to bring up what has been bound up, so it can open up to be freed up, and you can show up for Life.

> ❦ Close your eyes for a few moments and open into this living moment of your life. Hear it, sense it, feel it. This is the only moment that matters in your whole life for it is the only moment where Life is happening. ❧

Life Happens through You
The "Life happens for you" phase shows you that there is no such thing as an ordinary moment in your life and helps you see that Life is speaking to you at all moments. By becoming curious about what you are experiencing and giving it the light of compassionate attention so it can let go, you evolve into the next phase of allowing Life to move *through* you. This is where you recognize that Life is trustable. It is not always likable, but it knows what it is doing.

Imagine a life where you trust Life implicitly. Every morning you wake up with a sense of adventure. Your belly is soft, your mind is curious, and your heart is open. Rather than struggling with Life, you open to it, even when you are facing deep challenges. If you find yourself caught in reaction, you give your reaction the attention it needs to let go.

Just as when you unkink a hose, the vibrant flow of energy that is Life can now move freely through you, and this flow brings forth the joy and aliveness you so deeply long for. Creativity that you could never imagine on your own becomes clear to you, blessing you and everyone you meet with the wisdom of Life.

You experience deep gratitude for absolutely everything. You see that your life is dependent on every ounce of creativity that has ever happened in the universe. You also see that everything that has happened to you, even the difficult parts, has been a part of your journey back into Life. Step by step, Life is bringing you into consciousness, into the ability to be fully here for Life. Now you can relax and show up for the adventure. As Cynthia Bourgeault so beautifully says in her book *Mystical Hope,* "You find your way by being sensitively and sensually connected to exactly where you are, by letting 'here' reach out and lead you."

Life Is You
The more you allow Life to move through you rather than reacting to it or trying to control it, the more you glimpse the sixth phase, in which you see that Life *is* you. You are no longer a separate being. Instead, you merge completely into the creative flow of Life, understanding that everything—every rock, person, cloud, molecule, and ladybug—is you. You are Life! In the 2013 New World Library video "What Is the Divine Purpose of the Universe?" Eckhart Tolle said, "You're not *in* the universe, you *are* the universe, expressing itself through countless life forms . . . and with every experience, the universe is experiencing itself as your life . . . it wants to realize its own essence through you."

❮ All is well. Come here. ❯

*

As you look closely at the six phases of consciousness, you will see that the first two are about fixing, changing, resisting, and trying to control Life (Life is happening to you and by you). These phases are the world of your storyteller, which doesn't want what is here (doesn't know how to open to Life) and wants what is *not* here ("I can have what I want if I just think right"). Throughout both of these phases, there is a veil between you and the living experience of Life, because neither phase is about showing up for the creative flow of Life.

The next two phases of consciousness are about using your mind to be curious about what is happening rather than resisting and controlling. In the phase "Life is happening *in* you," you recognize that the storyteller inside you separates you from Life. So rather than trying to change anything, you become interested in what you are experiencing in any given moment. The more you are here for Life—the easy and the difficult, the joyous and the sorrowful—and the more you unhook from your spells, the clearer it becomes that Life knows what it is doing and that everything it is doing is *for* you.

The final two phases of consciousness are all about coming home to the meadow. The more you live the truth that Life is *for* you, the more you relax into the flow, which brings you to the joy of Life moving *through* you. As your clouds dissipate, you recognize the meadow again, and you also realize that you *are* the meadow. Life is you, and you are Life.

Most people live in the first two phases, "Life happens to you" and "Life happens by you," without knowing that right in the middle of these beliefs is a doorway into the last four. Life is waking you up from the contraction of the first two phases and into the openness of the last four. This is for your own healing and also for the healing of all beings, because as you see through your clouds of struggle, you become a healing presence in the world.

There is a paradoxical truth that is important to acknowledge. Human beings are evolving from the first phase to the sixth: "Life *is* you." It is also true that most days you will experience a number of these phases. It is not about getting rid of any particular phase or making one better than the other. They are all part of Life, and as you evolve, you will recognize and embrace them all.

THE TRUTH OF TRUST

In order to evolve into and through the last four phases, the tattered threads of your trust of Life need to be rewoven. You, like most people, probably don't trust Life. It certainly feels untrustworthy. Life breaks your heart, brings illness, and sometimes feels as if it gives you way more than you can handle. If you don't trust it, how can you show up for it? How can you open to all that it offers you in every experience you have? How can you allow it to bring you, step by step, from unconsciousness to consciousness? Shifting to the perception that Life is smarter than you will help you immensely in relearning that Life is something that can be opened to.

Most of us are so caught up in the words of our storyteller that we live in a small, tight world. All day long we pay attention to the clouds in our heads, which are made of our spells. We don't see what is going on. And we definitely don't recognize the meadow.

As a means of opening your awareness from this tight and small world, I invite you into what I call a "big-picture exploration." Imagine you are sitting on the moon, looking at the beautiful blue-green jewel that is our planet. See it as a living being that has been unfolding for 4.54 billion years. Look beyond it into the black, velvety depth of space, which is filled with more stars than there are grains of sand on every beach on Earth.

Now bring your attention back to the planet floating in front of you in space, and as you drink in its beauty, recognize that absolutely everything on this planet was created from atoms that come from the stars—and that includes you. So everything you see is made of stardust.

Now in your imagination, see the evolution of Earth as a movie. At its inception, the planet was just a ball of gas and dust. Fast-forward the movie in your mind's eye and see land and water appearing as Earth's atmosphere forms. Then see Life beginning to come together into various rudimentary beings in the seas. Now see Life crawl out of the seas and onto the continents as a wave of green flows across the formerly barren land. Insects appear, animals emerge, and dinosaurs come and go.

In the evolution of Life on this planet, there was a time when there were no creatures with opposable thumbs, so Life could not be picked up to be used and explored. Now see Life evolving a few million years ago into a form that had two arms with fingers and thumbs, and the kind of brain that was interested in picking up Life and exploring it. Life had never shown up in this way before.

Now see early human beings coming together into tribes. As their frontal lobes developed, see them discovering language, making tools, cultivating the land, building villages and towns, and then creating the wheel and ships that sail across oceans.

Fast-forward the movie again to just a few hundred years ago. See your great, great, great grandparents being born, growing up, discovering one another, giving birth, raising their family, and then disappearing back into mystery. This same cycle brought forth your grandparents, your parents, and then you. Now see yourself appearing out of mystery at the exact place on this planet where you were born. Watch yourself evolve from a baby, to a young child, to a teenager, and then to an adult.

As you are watching the movie of your life, bring it to this morning when you woke up, began your day, and eventually came to the moment when you are reading this book. Realize that all of the millions of moments of your life have unfolded to this moment, and this moment is the leading edge of the wave of evolution on this planet. Open to the knowing that this moment is no ordinary moment. Right here, right now, you are being given a very rare gift: the phenomenal gift of Life. For a short slice of time you get to be here, and then you too will dissolve back into mystery. And Life will continue to unfold.

꒷ Pause for a moment and contemplate all the creativity that has gone before you that allows you and everything around you to exist. ꒱

YOUR STORY

This movie about the unfolding of Life on this planet is *your* story. You are a being who is an expression of 4.54 billion years of Life evolving on this planet. You exist in this body because of the vast creativity that has gone before you. Let's take your eyes, for example. The first ancestors of your eyes came from polyps on the ocean floor that created cells that were able to differentiate light and dark.

In between that first rudimentary step into vision and your human ability to read this book are vast amounts of creativity. And it is not just your eyes that are dependent on the entire ingenuity of Life. Your whole life, like everybody else's, is dependent on every single act of creativity that has ever happened on this planet.

It is amazing to recognize the creativity that enabled Life to take stardust and make this planet and everything on it, including you. It is even more astounding to see that as you sit here reading this book, you are a community of seventy trillion cells that pump blood through 65,000 miles of arteries and veins, send messages along your nerves at the speed of light, regulate hormones, repair cells, and digest food without a single thought from you. If you doubt that there is an amazing Intelligence that permeates and penetrates all of Life, just acknowledge what is happening in your body right now.

Because you don't recognize the Intelligence at the heart of Life, you believe you are separate from it. Believing you are separate from it, you buy into the illusion that you must control it. As soon as you believe you must control it, you become cut off from it, losing sight of the joy of being open to Life.

You actually trust Life a lot. You trust it enough to beat your heart and keep your lungs filling with air, yet you think that the Intelligence at the heart of Life has nothing to do with your daily life. You, like most people, bought into the arrogance of the human ego that says that *it* is in charge. Because of this belief in separation, you think your life is just a random series of events that you must mold and shape into what you think they should be.

What would happen if this were not so? What would your life look like if you understood that the same Intelligence that keeps the planets spinning, heals the cuts on your skin, and brings forth spring out of winter is with you in every experience of your life? Can you open to the possibility that this creative Intelligence is weaving your life out of the primal opposites of dark and light, and that it is giving you exactly what you need in order to evolve from unconsciousness to consciousness? What would it be like if you understood that the same awesome force of evolution that created this planet and brought Life out of the sea and onto land is working its magic in your life?

To get even an inkling of what we are exploring here will allow you to let go of that grip of control enough that you can begin to feel the magic of trusting Life. The more you trust it, the more you will show up for it, and the more you show up for it, the more you will see that Life is wiser than you and is bringing you the exact set of experiences you need in order to come back to Life.

❦ Lift your eyes from the book and recognize that in the vastness of all time this moment will never be repeated and that you have the privilege to bear witness to it. ❧

WHAT IT LOOKS LIKE TO TRUST LIFE

When you realize that Life is smarter than you, your life becomes very interesting. Rather than being lost in your clouds of struggle, you realize something very extraordinary is happening here: there are no ordinary moments in your life. You become much more alert to what is happening, both outside and inside of you. Our lives are like icebergs; most people pay attention just to the part above water, but what is really going on happens underneath the water level of everyday awareness.

It is true that you are driving, working, showering, cooking, arguing, making love, raising children, birthing, and dying. But underneath it all is the unfolding of intelligent evolution, and you are part of that. You are evolving from an unconscious human being into a conscious one. This is happening in every experience of your life—*every* experience. Life is for Life. It is supporting your shift from being asleep to being awake. Just as Life assists a peach tree to create fruit by sustaining it with sun, rain, pollenating bees, and the nourishment of the earth, it is giving you exactly what you need to know the fruit of a conscious human being, which is the ability to be awake to Life.

Living from the truth that Life is for you, you begin to let go of the belief that your suffering is caused by something outside of you: other people, your job, the shape of your body, the kind of mate you have, the type of health you have, the kind of past you had, or the sort of mind you have. You begin to see that your suffering is coming from inside you, caused by the spells. Yes, there are difficult things that happen in your life, but when you don't get lost in your stories about them, you respond to the situation, gathering the gifts that are always embedded in the challenges of your life.

As you awaken, you become less interested in trying to change anything in your life and more interested in what is going on inside of you, especially in difficult situations. You have a deeper sense of allowing Life to put you in the exact situations you need in order for the core spells that make up your clouds to be brought to the surface of your awareness. It is there that you can see them, watch them in action, and discover that they are just spells that were conditioned into you when you were young, and that you no longer need to buy into them.

It is almost as if these deep and ancient spells are like champagne bubbles that have been trapped inside of you. As your resistance to experiencing them lessens, they loosen, arising to the surface to be seen. As they are fully seen, they burst, and the energy that was formerly trapped in them lets go. Rather than being afraid of this purification process, you begin to welcome it as the longing to be fully awake to Life becomes stronger than the fear of your spells.

> ❀ Pause for a moment and check into your belly.
> Allow any holding you discover there to melt away,
> and let a smile fill you with its healing presence.
> Allow this softening to move all the way down into
> your pelvic floor and around to your back. ❀

THE JOY OF RESPONSE-ABILITY

With any challenging situation in your life—illness, pain, a difficult neighbor, a compulsion, financial crisis, or anything else—it can be initially threatening to your storyteller to respond, rather than react, to what you are experiencing. Your storyteller feels it is responsible for its experience, so it must do something like fix, understand, or get rid of. There is a wonderful turn of phrase that opens us to the essence of what responsibility really is: "response-ability"—the ability to respond.

Old reactions that come from spells can be very strong, disrupting your ability to respond to the situation with curiosity. But you learn how to become like one of those three-foot-tall inflatable punching dolls with a weight in the bottom. When you're in a difficult situation, you may feel like the doll when it is punched and falls over. More and more quickly, however, you make a you-turn, becoming curious about what a situation is bringing up inside of you, and you bounce back up again, just like the punching doll does.

This is when you truly begin to trust Life. You know that difficult situations are *for* you. You see that just as the body cleanses itself of foreign viruses and bacteria through sweating, your being will cleanse itself of the old spells. The more you want to see your spells, the more Life puts you in situations that will bring them up, so they can be touched with the accepting attention of your heart and be free to let go. Thus, you are no longer the victim of your life.

In order to fully show up for Life, you will eventually have to meet the places within you that you are most afraid of. Remember the monster in the closet discussed in chapter 5? When you finally uncovered your eyes and looked at what you thought was a monster in your closet, you discovered it was a pile of clothing. In the same way, feelings, sensations, and stories become things to be curious about rather than feared. Even feelings like aloneness, unending sadness, or the black hole of nothingness, which seem so deep and real when you are resisting them, become something to say hello to and touch with compassion. As you listen to them, they no longer have the power over you they used to have, and the energy that was bound up in them is released, opening you to the meadow of your being.

As you are bringing consciousness into your daily life, it is important to remember that you have never left the meadow; you just think you have. All the joy, clarity, and aliveness you long for has always been with you, right here, right now. You just haven't seen it because your storyteller has grabbed your attention and rarely let it go. The more you allow Life to put you in the situations that bring up the core spells of your clouds, the more your clouds will thin and the more you will be able to recognize and live from the meadow of your being.

KEY POINTS

- Life is not a random series of events that happens because you did your life right or wrong. It is an intelligent unfolding that is always speaking to you, always waking you up.

- The first two phases of consciousness—"Life is happening to you" and "Life is happening by you"—are about fixing, changing, resisting, and trying to control Life. They put a veil between you and Life.

- The next two phases of consciousness are about curiosity. In "Life is happening in you," you become interested in what you are experiencing. In "Life is for you," you see that Life is putting you in the situations you need in order to see your spells.

- The final two phases of consciousness are all about coming home to the meadow. The more you relax into the flow of Life, the more you experience the joy of "Life happens through you." As you reconnect with the meadow again, you recognize that "Life is you."

- If you doubt the amazing Intelligence of Life, consider that you are made of seventy trillion cells working together, that your heart pumps blood through 65,000 miles of arteries and veins, and that your body heals cuts and digests food without a single thought from you.

- Because you don't recognize the Intelligence at the heart of Life, you believe you are separate from Life. Believing you are separate, you buy into the illusion that you must control it.

- To get even an inkling of what we are exploring here will allow you to let go of the grip of control enough that you can begin to feel the magic of trusting Life.

- Your spells are like champagne bubbles trapped inside of you. As your resistance lessens, they loosen, rising to the surface to be seen, so that the energy trapped in them can let go.

- Rather than being afraid of this process, you begin to welcome it, for the longing to come fully awake to Life is stronger than your fear of the spells.

- As you are able to more quickly do the you-turn, you truly begin to trust Life. You know that difficult situations are for you. You see that just as the body cleanses itself of foreign viruses and bacteria, your being will cleanse itself of the old spells.

-

-

-

REMEMBERING Week 9
This week's Remembering Statement:
Life is for me.
Your own statement:

Remembering Session

For this week's session, come back to the meadow metaphor. In the meadow everything flows, for everything is energy. The same is true for you. The energy of Life flows through you as feelings, sensations, and thoughts. The healing you long for comes when you allow Life to flow through you. You don't hold on to the comfortable and easy states, and you don't tighten around the uncomfortable and difficult.

All that you have been exploring in these Remembering Sessions has led you to this place where you can open up the field of your attention, and rather than identifying with your stories, feelings, and sensations, you become the space of awareness that allows all to simply pass through you.

We will begin with grounding your attention on your breath for just a few breaths, but then you will be invited to let go of your breath as a focus and allow curiosity to be your ground. This will feel a little bit like letting go of the steering wheel of a car. You are so used to trying to control Life that you may even be trying to control your Remembering Sessions. You may think a good session is when you stay on your focus and a bad one is when you don't. You are being invited to move beyond that perception and allow whatever is appearing to come and go without getting hooked by it. All is welcome here.

All sorts of things will arise inside of you and simply pass through you if you are curious. You will find that your attention will be drawn to your storyteller and the feelings and sensations that its stories generate, but then curiosity will naturally arise again. You may be lost in your clouds for a number of minutes, and then your natural curiosity will kick in again. If you don't judge yourself, you will be able simply to be curious about what is happening.

Remember, you are not trying to create any particular experience. Rather than trying to make something happen, or thinking about what is happening, or resisting it, or trying to change it, you are using your mind simply to be curious about what is going on right now. Your inner world is like the weather, and as you learn how to be curious, the weather of your stories, feelings, and sensations will pass through you like the clouds pass through the sky.

After you read the following section, put down the book, close your eyes, and begin exploring. If you are timing your session, set aside thirteen minutes. If time is not an issue, stay with each step as long as your curiosity is engaged.

Let's begin:

 ❦ Close your eyes and dip the finger of your attention into the river of your experience, noticing what it is like to be you right now.

For at least three in-breaths, tighten your muscles, and then very slowly relax everything on your out-breath as you say the great sound of letting go, *Ahh!*

For a few breaths, bring your attention to the circle of your breath, saying the calming/focusing words, "In . . . out. Deep . . . slow. Calm . . . ease. As is . . . I'm here." (Or say "As is . . . I'm here" by itself.)

Let go of paying attention to your breath and allow curiosity to be your ground.

Anything could be going on: different sensations in your body, stories in your head, emotions passing through. For these few precious moments, let go of trying to make something happen or needing things to be any different than they are, and just be interested. Let whatever is appearing arise and pass right through you.

In the beginning of your session, your mind may wander. You may think about the day or feel scared that you are not doing the session right. But if you stay open, your natural curiosity will kick in, and you will be interested in what is showing up inside of you. It can help to ask yourself throughout the session, "What am I paying attention to right now?" Be curious about what is before you think about it.

If you find your mind wandering a lot, ground in your breath for a few breaths, and then open up the field of your attention again and be curious about what is sitting here right now. Stay with this curiosity as long as the mind is willing. It may be for thirty seconds or thirty minutes.

When you are ready, open your eyes. ⸙

Abbreviated Version

⸙ Close your eyes and check in, noticing what it is like to be you right now.

For at least three in-breaths, tighten your muscles, and then very slowly relax everything on your out-breath as you say the great sound of letting go, *Ahh!*

For a few breaths, bring your attention to the circle of your breath, saying the calming/focusing words, "In . . . out. Deep . . . slow. Calm . . . ease. As is . . . I'm here." (Or say "As is . . . I'm here" by itself.)

Let go of riding the waves of your breath and open the field of your attention. Be curious about what is showing up inside of you, allowing whatever is here to be here.

If you find your mind wandering a lot, ground in your breath for a few breaths, and then open up the field of your attention again and be curious about what is sitting here right now.

When you are ready, open your eyes. ⸙

10

The Song of the Heart

Will your clouds of struggle dissolve all of a sudden when you recognize what is being offered in this book? That has not been my experience or the experience of 99.999 percent of the people I have known over the years. It is, as Stephen Levine once described it, a gradual awakening. When asked by someone how long this would take, he responded by saying, "This is the work of a lifetime."

You will remember and forget, contracting and expanding on a daily basis, just like your heart valve opens and closes and your breath flows in and out. One day you will be very clear, easily letting go of any story of struggle. Then the next day you may fall into a story that feels like it always has and always will have you in its grip. But remember, you are putting together the picture puzzle of all of the stories in your head so you can unhook from your storyteller's spells, and every moment of relating *to* what you are experiencing rather than relating *from* it truly matters.

Once you see that you are in the meadow right now and it is only your clouds of struggle that keep you from knowing it, you will become more and more curious, in a compassionate way, about whatever you are experiencing. You will also remember to turn your challenges over to Life, so the wisdom at the heart of Life can guide and support you. This will lead you to the place where you can simply be open to Life, entering its flow, knowing more and more ease and joy.

THE FOUR LETS

It is helpful to condense all that we have explored into what I call the "Four Lets," which will help you respond clearly and cleanly to whatever level of opening or closing is happening.

- Let Life.
- Let it be.
- Let it go.
- Let go.

"Let Life" is a doorway out of the core reactions of your storyteller through the art of turning your challenges over to Life, allowing the Intelligence of Life to support you every step of the way.

This opens you into the curiosity of "Let it be," which is about not fighting your experience so that in that spaciousness you can explore what is going on. This allows you to bring the healing of your compassionate attention to your spells, which helps them let go.

With "Let it go," you come to a place where you can simply let go of many of your spells when they arise. You have given them enough curiosity and compassion that they pass through you rather than getting caught in their stories.

This brings you to "Let go," which is when your clouds of struggle have been thinned enough that you are able to rest in the meadow of your being. Opening to this moment, you relax into Life, allowing it to flow through you, as you.

If you look carefully, there is a progression of consciousness in the Four Lets, starting with "Let Life," which helps immensely when you are caught in your storyteller, and progressing all the way to "Let go," where you are fully open to Life. Let us take time to explore each in depth.

Let Life

There will be many times in your life when reaction will take over so fast that you won't have a clue about what is going on inside you. You will be caught in your clouds, feeling there is no way out of the morass of feelings and stories that are flooding through you. There also will be times when you can see you are caught because you are tightening around a situation, but you don't know what is going on inside and you feel resistance to making the you-turn and looking. Finally, there will be times when you use the tools of consciousness and your resistance only gets tighter.

When you are this contracted, it is very easy to get seduced into your spells: "I am not doing Life right." "This is going to last forever." "I am not enough." "What is wrong with me that this keeps on happening?" When this contraction happens, there will be an almost magnetic attraction to falling into the spells. It will feel as though almost everything inside of you wants to buy into the spells, but if you have followed that path enough times in your life, you will remember that it only leads to more suffering.

This is the time to open into "Let Life." The first gift that comes from "Let Life" is the art of acknowledging you are caught and feeling powerless in the face of the reactions inside. Rather than being completely lost in reaction, you consciously acknowledge that you are caught. This may not seem like much, but it is a powerful moment of consciousness within the clouds of spells. The ability to say, "I see that I am caught in reaction," allows you to take a half-step out of the morass of struggle.

The second part of "Let Life" is the willingness to ask Life for clarity. No matter how stormy the clouds are, you have never left the meadow. It is always with you, no matter what is happening in your life, and it can be accessed simply by asking for help from the Intelligence that is Life.

Remember, this kind of asking isn't looking for an answer. That just keeps you caught in your head. To ask Life an open-ended question, such as "What is asking to be met?" or "What is the way through this?" or "What am I ready to see?" creates an opening so that the answers can live themselves through you in Life's time and in Life's way. Every moment of asking counts, especially when it doesn't seem like anything is happening.

❧ Allow one long, deep breath and contemplate the
possibility that you are not living the dance of Life alone. ❧

Let It Be

As you awaken, there will be more and more moments when you become interested in what is going on inside you when you are in reaction, contraction, or just not available to Life. You become willing to do the you-turn, turning your attention toward yourself with the intention of allowing whatever is happening to be there. This is the next *Let*, "Let it be," and it is about not resisting what is happening, so that your reactions can calm down. Then it becomes easier to see and become available to what is going on inside of you.

It is in this space of allowing things to be as they are that alchemy happens, for the truth of spells is that they are like people. If you try to fix them, deny them, judge them, or get rid of them, they resist you back. When you are willing to acknowledge the spells and listen to their view of the world, they feel heard, and feeling heard dramatically increases the chances that when you are ready to let go of a spell, it will let go.

The default mode of your storyteller, which is resistance, is the opposite of allowing, which is at the heart of "Let it be." But remember what we explored in chapters 5 and 6: trying to get away from what you are experiencing only increases the struggle of your storyteller. If you turn toward what you're experiencing with curiosity, you now have some space around it, and it is spaciousness (the opposite of reaction) that heals.

Allowing is key here, for you can't really look and listen to something if you are resisting its presence. Allowing comes from the understanding that embedded in all of your reactions to Life are spells waiting for your willingness to be with them so they can let go. One of the clearest ways to describe "Let it be" is the ability to say, "For just this moment, I am going to allow whatever is happening inside of me to be there so I can bring my attention to it."

Allowing trusts that Life is for Life. Allowing knows that everything that tightens us is a growth opportunity. There is nothing to be afraid of or ashamed of. There is just something to be opened to, explored, and seen for what it is: blocked energy that makes up the spells. Allowing opens a door so you can show up for your own life experiences and give them the attention they need to let go.

Let's take anxiousness as an example. Imagine that this is a feeling you have known a lot in your life. Every time it appears, you feel resistant, overwhelmed, and desperate to get out of this feeling. But if you are honest, you know whatever you do to get out of the feeling may bring temporary relief, but it doesn't bring the lasting freedom from anxiousness you long for. Through "Let it be," you turn your attention toward it, being curious about whatever you are experiencing that causes you to say you are anxious. If you stay with this exploration, anxiousness itself will let go, and if it arises again, you will be less afraid of it, so it will pass through much more quickly.

Sometimes it is hard to access the power of letting something be. You have been so trained to resist and control. To accept your immediate experience so you can explore it, it helps to relate to this experience as if you had chosen it. Imagine what it would be like to have the flu and be miserable all day long. Then imagine shifting your relationship with it by saying, "This is a part of my awakening. Rather than resisting it, I choose to be with it." With this kind of spaciousness, your experience of the flu would be completely different.

If that doesn't work, imagine that Life has chosen it for you—that this is where destiny has placed you, and your job is to bring your conscious attention to it. This perspective allows whatever suffering you are experiencing to be transformed back into the free-flowing aliveness that is who you really are.

Both of these shifts of perception take you out of the victim mode of unconsciousness and open you into the power of consciously looking at whatever you are experiencing, which is what "Let it be" is all about.

> ❧ Pause for a moment and sing the Beatles song "Let It Be." Linger on the wisdom of the title and chorus phrase: "Let it be." ❧

Let It Go
As you become more able to see your spells through the first two *Lets* ("Let Life" and "Let it be"), it becomes easier to see and unhook from

a spell when it arises. This brings you to "Let it go," which is the place where you soften around a spell and simply let it pass through you.

Let's take the feeling of being anxious again. Now that you have explored it through "Let it be" rather than identifying with the spell by saying, "I am anxious," you can see it as a pattern of belief that was conditioned inside of you. You then become able to say, "This is just anxiousness, and I don't need to tighten around it." You are not interested in following the storyline of anxiety or resisting its energy. So you simply let it go and bring your attention back to Life. Remember, you are not the spells. They were just conditioned into you when you were young. Instead, you are that which can see the spells, and the more you watch them, the more they lose their power over you.

Sometimes it is difficult to let go of a spell, but the more you see the alchemy that happens when you bring your full attention to the bound-up energy of a spell, the more you recognize that there is no spell that is worth closing around. If you do close, you can see clearly that in doing so you lock this spell inside and bind up your joy in the process. There comes a time when nothing is worth closing around. You want to stay open to Life more than you want to identify with the seductiveness of your spells.

Unhooking from a spell is one of the most joyous experiences of Life, and just a little bit of unhooking goes a long way. Yes, there is a very deep urge to tighten around your spells. Make it a passion to recognize those spells and relax, letting them pass through you rather than fighting them. You have been taught to identify with your spells for most of your life, so the tendency to get drawn in is strong, but the willingness to not get caught in the drama of the spells becomes stronger the more you develop your capacity for compassionate curiosity. As you let your life be about allowing whatever happens to make it through you, you will know your natural state of joy.

᚜ Let go of reading and bring your attention to your breath. On the next in-breath, tighten your muscles, and on the out-breath, slowly let go. Do as many letting go breaths as you like, and then smile. ᚛

Let Go

Through "Let Life," "Let it be," and "Let it go," you thin your clouds of spells enough to discover the safety and the joy of being here for Life, not an idea of it but the living experience of it. This brings you to the fourth *Let:* "Let go," the joy of relaxing into Life. With "Let go," you remember to stay open to Life rather than trying to control or manipulate it. You recognize that the great river of Life has been unfolding long before you came here and will continue on long after you have left. You also realize that Life happens. You don't make it happen. You learn to step back and bear witness to its unfolding. The way Pema Chödrön defines awakening is appropriate here: "Relaxing into life!"

These two little words, "Let go," capture the essence of what this book is about, and they are a wonderful mantra for Life. With "Let go," you open to the natural unfolding of Life rather than using your mind to protect yourself from it. When you do start becoming tight, simply saying "Let go" dissolves whatever struggle your storyteller is caught in.

Instead of being open to Life, you were conditioned to be afraid of it, believing that your job was to control it and make it be what you thought it should be. This only causes you to live tight and small. You are so busy trying to do the next thing right that you can't be here with Life. If you are honest with yourself, you will see that trying to make the unknown known, so you can stay in the illusion of control, has never brought you the lasting peace you long for.

A Tibetan lama told Andrew Harvey, author and teacher of mystic traditions, that once you see what is going on here, you will nearly die laughing. We have been trying to control the uncontrollable, keeping ourselves tied up in knots. We all have been like gnats on the back of an elephant trying to control the elephant and feeling very frustrated that it never quite works out. When you finally stop trying to control Life and instead show up for the ride, you discover that this is where the joy is. Even the greatest of challenges now opens you back into the meadow of your being.

Instead of staying tight and small in a mind that is based on fear, it is time to expand and open, discovering that the safest thing you will ever do is show up for the life you have been given. This can be scary, for you have been caught for a long, long time in a conceptual world believing that your mind was in charge of Life. In giving itself this impossible task, your mind has, like most minds, become self-absorbed and neurotic. It is not fun to be lost in the struggle of your storyteller, which focuses mainly on itself all day long. When you realize that Life is smarter than you, you can expand back into Life.

Most people, caught in their fear of Life, believe their minds are more powerful than Life. But I ask you, do you beat your heart? Did you create your eyes? Do you bring forth spring out of winter? Do you heal the cuts on your skin? No, the forces of Life create and orchestrate your life, and Life is trustable. Yes, it includes death, illness, and loss, but the suffering you experience by not trusting it, by not opening to it, is far greater than any pain you will experience as you stay open to it all, even to the difficult parts.

Upon discovering that Life is smarter than you and knows what it is doing, you no longer live exclusively in your mind. That doesn't mean that you don't use the mind; it means the mind no longer uses you, cutting you off from Life with its endless game of struggle. Your mind is an exquisite tool to help you maneuver through your life, but its thoughts about Life are not Life. Your mind's true function is to be fully here for Life, not to control it.

> ❋ Let go of reading for a few moments and simply open to Life. Recognize that whatever is happening right now has never happened on this planet before. It is totally brand new. Rather than thinking about it, just receive it. Drink it in. It is safe to let yourself go to the great river of Life. ❋

You are homesick for this. You are homesick for fully participating in the great unfolding of Life that is happening right now as you are reading this book. Life is giving you the gift of Life, and for this moment, you get to bear witness to it. The flow of events that is your life is unique to you, and one day you won't be here to experience it anymore. Life will keep on unfolding, but you will be gone. Out of this recognition comes a passion to listen deeply to whatever your attention is drawn to in any moment—the song of a bird, a delicious meal, a pain in your belly, a person who is in joy, a person who is suffering, fear in your mind, your death—for *this is your life.*

In your passion for Life, you no longer want to resist the flow of events that is at the heart of "Let go." Instead, you allow more and more moments of the day to pass through you. Anthony de Mello, the Jesuit priest and psychotherapist, called it "absolute cooperation with the inevitable." What gives Life its richness is the willingness to live it. Embrace it rather than resisting it. Live your life! Joy arises out of embracing every experience. The only way you can become this open is to realize that everything on this planet is impermanent, including the planet. People, animals, events, and experiences all die. It is natural for everything that appears to eventually disappear back into mystery. So be willing to die into Life.

The more you "Let go" to Life, the more available you become to it. There arises an intimacy between you and Life. Rather than a series of problems to be solved, Life becomes a dance of discovery, and the simplest of things have deeply profound effects on you. With great joy, you discover that the more you are okay with what is, the more you see that everything is okay. There is a sense of ease and a willingness to let go of the part that is afraid of what will happen next.

Trusting this great mystery of Life, you are willing to be blind about the future. You realize that anything is possible and nothing is certain. You recognize that your mind can never know what is going to happen next, but that is okay because you know the greatest gift a human can know: the ability to be with Life as it is right now. Instead of thinking and planning your way through Life, you discover how to feel for the energies. There are currents flowing through Life, and you learn how to let these forces move you. In feeling your way through your life, your storyteller becomes quieter, and your heart becomes the guiding force.

My book *The Magical Forest of Aliveness* is an exploration of the journey back to Life that we have been exploring. It is a fairy tale for adults (although many people have told me their children love it, too) about a little girl named Rose, who gets caught behind the walls of the village called Mind. She eventually finds her way out of the village and back into the magical forest of aliveness, where, in a beautiful clearing deep in the woods, she rediscovers who she really is. Then a lion, a tiger, and a bear teach her about consciousness and how to be open to Life.

When it is time to go back to the village, her old fears suddenly rise up to the surface: "I can't be open to Life. That sounds like I will be doing nothing. Besides, I will just be a doormat! Either bad things will happen, or nothing will happen." Now, however, Rose can feel how these thoughts are tightening her rather than opening her, and she is able to unhook from their stories.

As she looks across the field toward the village, the words "Don't know" come to her as a healing balm. When she was caught in the village of Mind, those words created fear and frustration, but now they come from the Intelligence of Life. "I truly don't know what will happen in my life, and I don't need to know. My life will unfold the way it needs to. Having to know kept me caught in my head. Not needing to know keeps me open to the great mystery of Life."

> ❮ Close your eyes for a few moments, allowing in a deep breath. Then on a long, slow out-breath, say, "Don't know." Stretch the words out so they last for your whole out-breath. Breathe this "don't know" breath as many times as it calls to you. ❯

*

Through the Four Lets, we have been exploring the most important choice a human being has: the choice to use the mind to control or to connect. In fact, this is the only true choice you have. It is either mind or moment. You either give your attention to all the stories and spells in your head that make up your clouds of struggle, or you allow your life to unfold, giving it your passionate and compassionate attention, interacting with it in a natural way. There will always be challenges, but Life is a lot easier when you relax into it enough to dance with Life, rather than living from your spells.

LIVING FROM YOUR HEART

All that we have explored allows the wisdom of your heart, rather than your mind, to become the guiding force in your life. Life shows up differently when you discover how to listen to your heart. Remember in chapter 7 when you were invited to imagine somebody you deeply love, and you were able to feel how the energy in your chest shifts? It expands, opens, and even glows. You were also able to see that if you stayed with the feeling of deep love long enough, your whole body would glow. Every cell in your body responds to the radiance of an open heart. So, too, do the different parts of yourself, your loved ones, strangers, plants, and animals. They all thrive when touched by an open heart.

What does it look like when the heart is your guiding force? There is openness, for the heart doesn't divide and separate like the mind does. The words that describe a heart-focused Life are *allowing, spaciousness, curiosity, playfulness, spontaneity,* and *trust.* As your mind drops into your heart, you value being real, speaking truth, not fighting what is, responding rather than reacting, being curious about what is, having times of quiet and stillness, not asserting your position, and listening and appreciating your life just the way it is. And when you live a heart-oriented life, you thrive in the meadow of your natural okayness and become a healing force in the world.

The more your mind gets enfolded by your heart, the more you begin to experience Life in ways that you have longed for: with an ease in loving and being loved, the joy of seeing Love everywhere, and a deep gratitude for even the smallest of things. We have explored that the essence of our existence is Love, but because we don't see this, we are starving. We are like fish in the ocean thirsty for water, so our whole life becomes a search for Love. All you have to do is listen to the lyrics of most popular songs and you will hear how starved we are.

Courage means "of the heart," and discovering the courage to look at your spells allows you to discover the power of your own heart and to recognize that the love affair you have longed for your whole life is with yourself. When you are able to open your heart to all of you, so that there is no spell, sensation, feeling, or thought inside you that cannot be included in your heart, then your body and mind will glow with the energy of Love.

No love from outside of you will ever fully satisfy you, because the only way to relieve that longing is to know who you truly are. The love you receive from another human being is only a drop in the bucket compared to the depth of Love you can become when you realize you *are* Love. You arise from the energy that animates everything. Every atom that makes up every cell in your body is filled with light, and the activity of that light is Love. To step out of the struggles of your storyteller and rest in the field of Love is to experience the radiance that you truly are.

Then an amazing thing begins to happen. Rather than the suffering of endlessly searching for love, you begin to realize that the greatest joy of Life is to *be* this Love. In realizing that your destiny is to be Love, another wondrous shift begins to happen. You tap into the great circle of giving and receiving that is Love. The more you give Love, the more it comes back to you, and you recognize it everywhere.

This Love then expands to include all of humanity. You recognize there is only one of us here, and we are all in this together. You see that Life is like a mighty tree with billions of leaves. Each person is a leaf, and we are all on the same tree, connected by the same roots. Looking out of everybody's eyes is the same animating Presence that permeates all of Life.

Most people you meet don't see this about themselves, and so they maneuver through Life caught in their spells, which causes their light to dim. But through the eyes of your heart, you can see who they truly are. A Christmas song called "Mary, Did You Know?" written by Mark Lowry and Buddy Greene, asks whether the Virgin Mary knew that she "kissed the face of God" when she kissed the baby Jesus. It is wonderful to see the face of God in baby Jesus, but when you wake up to the truth of Love, you see the face of God in everyone.

When living from your heart, you are automatically open to everyone, and you give them the fullness of your presence, whether it is a grocery store clerk, a person in the car next to you during a traffic jam, or your loved one. It doesn't matter how deeply caught they are in their spells. It doesn't matter that they, like all human beings, have done unskillful things in their lives and maybe even have hurt you in their unskillfulness. You realize that they are doing the best they know how while caught in the conditioning of their spells. Relating to others from your heart and allowing the truth of their being to shine out of your eyes helps to thin their clouds of struggle. You then become a force of consciousness in the world.

This kind of Love also expands to include all of Life. You recognize that the source of every single thing is the same: the Intelligence at the heart of Life. Just as people are like leaves on the tree of Life, all nourished by the same source, so too is every single form. It doesn't matter whether it is a person, a feeling, a thought, a plant, an insect, a rock, grass, a dolphin, a star, or your child. All are brought forth out of mystery and are animated by the same energy, and all deserve to be met with the spaciousness, inclusion, and acceptance of the heart. This is when you step into your true essence: a lover of what is.

It does appear that there are separate forms, but you see the interconnectedness at the same time, for everything is linked to and nourished by the roots of the tree of Life, which is Love. Every single expression of Life is like a cell in your heart. Yes, the cell is a separate entity, but it would not exist without the community of the heart. And the heart would not exist without the greater community of a body, and the body would not exist without the whole community of Life.

When you live from the heart, you swim in a sea of gratitude, not taking anything for granted. You are grateful for everything: for the food that the earth gives you every day (and all the forces it takes to make this happen), for the amazing gift of a body that allows you to experience Life through the senses, for your senses themselves (what would it be like to be unable to see or hear?), for the ability to walk (many people can't do this). You even discover how to be grateful for the challenges in your life because you recognize they are clearing your spells so that you can be fully here for Life. There is practically no greater joy a human being can know than living from gratitude.

The experience of seeing everything—rivers, people, the seasons, your body, your challenges—as the outpouring of Love is all about coming home to your heart. When Life becomes something to love rather than to possess, you are moved beyond feeling separate and alone, for your heart weaves you back into the very fabric of Life. This then becomes your passion: to show up for Life and experience it through your heart. Everything else is secondary in relationship to this willingness to be available to Life with an open heart. And when you are cut off again, caught in your spells, you now know how to bring Love to them.

> ❦ See Earth in your imagination and allow yourself to be moved by her beauty—the green of her mountains, the blue of the oceans, the gold of her fields. Now see the billions of people who are right now walking, driving, sleeping, working, birthing, dying, laughing, crying. See that most of them have clouds swirling around their heads, blocking their view of Life.
>
> Now see a human being who has become free from her clouds standing in front of a person who hasn't, touching that second person with her heart. Watch this heart energy dissipate the second person's clouds so that he or she is again available to Life. Now see both of these people turning to two other people and meeting them with the healing of the heart. Watch this spread all over the planet as more and more people come out of their clouds of struggle and live from the meadow of their being. Know that your life is a part of this healing process that is happening now on our planet. ❧

TRUSTING THE PROCESS

You don't have to try to find your heart, for it is always here. It has just been hidden because of the storyteller's endless addiction to struggle. Trying to find your heart is just one more cloud. The healing you are ready for doesn't come from changing anything. It comes from the willingness to be curious about what is right now, in a spacious way, so your clouds can thin, and, *voilà*, there is the meadow of your being.

Yes, this takes patience, which is not a strong quality of the storyteller. The definition of patience is "quiet, steady perseverance;

even-tempered care." As one of the teachers I highly respect once said, "The three most important words in awakening are 'Just keep walking.'"

For most of us, our awakening will be slow and steady, hardly noticeable in comparison to the noisy voice of the storyteller in our heads, but it is there nonetheless. Awakening is similar to what happens at the beginning of the day: there isn't an instant appearance of light. Instead, there is a gradual shift from the dark of night to the first fingerlings of light. The stars slowly disappear as the light of day fully appears.

So don't expect instant awakening, but know that Life is waking you up. If it weren't, you wouldn't be interested in what is being offered here. Ramana Maharshi, one of the most respected teachers of awakening, once said that all you need is the willingness to awaken. Because you are reading this book, the willingness is already here. So no matter what your life looks like, Life is waking you up, step by step, bringing you out of the suffering of struggle and back into Life.

You can trust the flow of Life. It is for you. The same Intelligence that has shaped the unfolding of Life from the beginning of time—creating stars, forming the earth, and bringing you forth out of mystery—is what is breathing you right now. It is only one step more to recognize that the same Intelligence is in charge of the unfolding of your life. The meadow of your being will not fail you. It is working tirelessly to bring you back, step by step, into recognition of who you truly are.

The more you trust Life, the more you show up for your own life. The most meaningful relationship you will ever have is your willingness to be in relationship with what Life is giving you. The more you are willing to be curious and accepting, the more you will discover that the path to your freedom is the ground beneath your feet, for what is in the way *is* the way. Be willing to be curious about what is right now, and Life will guide you home. Then you will become the fullness of what human beings have been brought forth to experience: the consciousness that can celebrate and bear witness to the amazing creation called Life.

KEY POINTS

- You will remember and forget, contracting and expanding on a daily basis, just like your heart valve opens and closes and your breath flows in and out.

- "Let Life" is the art of turning your challenges over to Life and allowing the Intelligence of Life to support you every step of the way.

- "Let it be" is all about not fighting what you are experiencing, so that in spaciousness you can explore what is going on, bringing it the healing of your heart.

- In "Let it go," you come to a place where you can simply let go of many of your spells when they arise. Make it a passion of your life to recognize your spells and let them pass through you.

- In "Let go," you relax into Life, allowing it to flow through you. Rather than using your mind to protect yourself from the natural unfolding of Life, you open to it.

- The more you let go to Life, the more available you become. Rather than a series of problems to be solved, Life becomes a dance of discovery.

- All that we have explored allows the wisdom of your heart to become the guiding force in your life. The words that describe a heart-focused life are *allowing, spaciousness, curiosity, playfulness, spontaneity,* and *trust.*

- Your body will glow with the energy of Love when you are able to open your heart to all of yourself so that there is no spell, sensation, feeling, or thought inside of you that cannot be included in your heart.

- There is only one of us here, and we are all in this together. Life is like a tree with billions of leaves. Each person is a leaf on that tree, connected by the same roots, and looking out of everybody's eyes is the same animating Presence that permeates all of Life.

- Everybody and everything deserves to be met with the spaciousness, the inclusion, and the acceptance of the heart. This is when you step into your true essence: a lover of what is.

- Don't expect awakening to appear instantly, but know that Life is waking you up.

- You can trust the flow of Life. It is for you. The same Intelligence that shaped the unfolding of Life from the beginning of time, that created stars, that formed our beautiful home we call Earth, and that brought you forth out of mystery is breathing you right now.

-

-

-

REMEMBERING   Week 10
This week's Remembering Statement:
I welcome Life as it is right now.
Your own statement:

Remembering Session

You have spent nine weeks dipping the finger of your attention into the river of your experience, discovering how to meet yourself right where you are by quieting your mind and opening your heart. This session will include the standard pathway we have been developing, or you may find your own pathway this week if you are called to do so. Whether you develop your own or stay with the pathway we have been exploring, we will then add one more step to this session. If you are timing your session, set aside fourteen minutes.

If you are going to create your own pathway, following is a list of the skills we have explored through the previous chapters. If you are called to use the suggested pathway I have outlined, skip the next two sections and go to the paragraph on page 224 title "Suggested Pathway."

Skills We Have Explored

- On your in-breath, tighten every muscle in your body. Then very slowly relax everything on your out-breath as you say the great sound of letting go, *Ahh!*

- Open to the letting in of the in-breath and the letting go of the out-breath. As you ride the waves of breath, say silently to yourself, "In . . . out. Deep . . . slow."

- Lengthen your out-breath by first breathing in through your nostrils and then gently blowing out through your mouth. As you become comfortable with a longer out-breath, breathe in and out through your nostrils.

- As you ride the circle of your breath, whenever you find yourself paying attention to your storyteller again, notice if you are telling yourself stories about the past or the future. If your stories are about the past, say, "Past." If you notice your stories are about the future, say, "Future." If you can't immediately see past or future, or if you are just spacing out, say, "Story." Then bring your attention back to the circle of your breath.

- Explore your body by bringing your attention to a familiar place of holding in your body. Rather than turning away from it, turn toward it, being curious about what is happening in this area. Sensations will gradually reveal themselves through the light of your attention, just like a Polaroid picture developing.

- Say "As is" on the in-breath and "I'm here" on the out-breath, reminding yourself to embrace all the parts of your being so they can receive the nourishment of your compassionate attention.

- Bring your attention to the circle of your breath, saying the calming/focusing words, "In . . . out. Deep . . . slow. Calm . . . ease. As is . . . I'm here."

- Discover your own set of words to say on the rhythm of your breath.

- Whenever you notice that you are no longer fully with your breath, notice what has captured your attention. Say to the feeling/sensation/story, "I see you," and then let it go, bringing your attention back to your breath.

- When your attention has drifted away from the circle of your breath, ask yourself, "What is asking to be seen?" If you notice a feeling/sensation/story, explore it with the finger of your attention. Say to whatever you are noticing, "I see you. It is okay that you are here. Tell me about your world." These words are inviting you to be fully with whatever is there without falling into it, giving it the healing of your own heart.

- Allow curiosity to be your ground so you can sit with feelings/sensations/stories that arise and let them pass right through you.

Creating Your Own Pathway

In customizing your personal pathway, listen to yourself and discover what works best for you. Play with what calls to you. As you continue to give yourself the gift of daily quiet time, know that your pathway can live and breathe. One day you may stay with the circle of your breath the whole time. Another day you will be grounded and spacious enough that you hardly need to anchor to your breath. On another, it will interest you to explore what is drawing your attention away from your breath, and the next day all you may be able to do is turn it over to Life. Always use your breath as your initial ground and then go from there.

At the end of your session:

≮ Open your eyes and fully receive this moment of your life. See it with new eyes as if you have never seen it before. All of the millions of moments of your life have brought you here, and this moment will never be the same again. Drink it in. Let go of any filters between you and this living moment so you can rest in the great river of Life.

Note that fear may come. Your mind is afraid of letting go of control, for it has forgotten that something else is in charge, that all of Life is made out of Love and every single experience is for you. Open to Life and discover that this is the safest thing you will ever do, for this moment is your home.

When you are ready, open your eyes. ≯

Suggested Pathway

≮ Close your eyes and dip the finger of your attention into the river of your experience, noticing what it is like to be you right now.

For at least three in-breaths, tighten your muscles, and then very slowly relax everything on your out-breath as you say the great sound of letting go, *Ahh!*

For a few breaths, bring your attention to the circle of your breath, saying the calming/focusing words, "In . . . out. Deep . . . slow. Calm . . . ease. As is . . . I'm here." (Or, you can say, "As is . . . I'm here" by itself.)

Let go of paying attention to your breath and allow curiosity to be your ground, allowing feelings/sensations/stories to arise and pass through you.

If you find your attention wandering, come back to the circle of your breath and stay with it as long as it feels right, even if it is the whole time. Trust where you are. The more you discover you don't need to control your experience, the greater the chances are that you will be able to expand your attention beyond your breath and be curious, allowing the energy of feelings/sensations/stories to move through you.

At the end of your session, open your eyes and fully receive this moment of your life. See it with new eyes as if you have never seen it before. All of the millions of moments of your life have brought you here, and this moment will never be the same again. Drink it in. Let go of any filters between you and this living moment so you can rest in the great river of Life.

Note that fear may come. Your mind is afraid of letting go of control for it has forgotten that something else is in charge—that it is all made out of Love and every single experience is for you. Open to it and discover that this is the safest thing you will ever do, for this moment is your home.

When you are ready, open your eyes. ❦

Abbreviated Version

❦ Close your eyes and dip the finger of your attention into the river of your experience, noticing what it is like to be you right now.

For at least three in-breaths, tighten your muscles, and then very slowly relax everything on your out-breath as you say the great sound of letting go, *Ahh!*

Bring your attention to the circle of your breath, saying the calming/focusing words, "In . . . out. Deep . . . slow. Calm . . . ease. As is . . . I'm here." (Or say, "As is . . . I'm here" by itself.)

Let go of paying attention to your breath and allow curiosity to be your ground, allowing feelings/sensations/stories to arise and pass through you.

If you find your attention wandering, come back to the circle of your breath for a few breaths, and then open the field of your attention again and be curious about what sits here right now.

At the end of your session, open your eyes and receive this moment of your life with new eyes. ❧

Conclusion

Awakening for Life

Everything we have been exploring together—the truth of the meadow of your being, how your storyteller keeps you separate from what is truly going on, and that you can live from the meadow when you recognize and see through the spells you took on—is all opening you again to the creative flow of Life. This is about saying "yes" to Life. That doesn't mean that you sit down by the side of the road and let it run you over. It means that at your core you know that everything in your life is for you: it is not just a random series of events. Life is an intelligent process. It knows what it is doing, and opening to it is safe.

Opening to Life brings you into full engagement with what is happening rather than keeping you caught in a conversation about Life. We could call it surrender, but this doesn't mean being defeated. It means finally giving up your war with what Life is bringing you. We could also call it humility, but the dictionary misses this word's full meaning when it defines it as "lowliness, meekness, submissiveness." True humility is a state of great availability. From this kind of openness, you finally realize how smart Life is. Openness fosters a shift from the mind that tries to control to the heart that connects.

Can Life be trusted? Alan W. Watts, the celebrated philosopher, author, and teacher, once said, "To the individual thus enlightened it appears as a vivid and overwhelming certainty that the universe, precisely as it is at this moment, as a whole and in every one of its parts, is so completely right, as to need no explanation or justification, beyond what it simply is." In other words, it is safe to open to Life!

Opening to the way things actually are, rather than always trying to make Life be what you think it should be, is the most courageous and healing thing you can do. When you see through the game of struggle enough so that the veils between you and this living moment—this miraculous, incandescent moment—lift, you become a healing presence in the world. Moments of full connection with Life matter. In fact, they matter more than you can possibly know. They are what will heal our world.

The struggling mind has been the dominant force on this planet for too long. When it is in charge, people literally value feeling separate and thus buy into the world of fear, believing that the only way to work with Life is to be in control. We have all believed this so strongly that we are sure that if we don't control Life, we will die. This belief breeds conflict, efforting, blaming, anxiety, resistance, compulsions, defensiveness, one-upmanship, and judgment.

In his video series *Canticle to the Cosmos,* author and evolutionary cosmologist Brian Swimme speaks directly to how deeply the clouds of struggle in our heads have taken over most human beings and how important it is that we see through them and open again to the amazing creative flow of Life. When he uses the word *sacred,* he is referring to the recognition of the mysterious, magical creation that is unfolding in every moment of Life.

> Something very basic within the human body, the human mind, the human sensitivity has closed down. The sacred dimension has been lost sight of. Our way out of our difficulty is the journey into the universe as sacred. It is activating the sensitivity of the human that responds to the sacred dimension of the universe. It is a regeneration of the human spirit, enabling it once again to tremble with awe before these naked mysteries. What awaits us is the unfurnished eye . . . meaning seeing what is before us.
>
> We don't see what is before us. Our trouble as a species is that we don't know where we are. We don't know what surrounds us. We don't know what's about us. We don't know what

we are about. The task is to initiate ourselves into the universe, into this enveloping mystery, a region of delight and excitement.

The greatest mission you can undertake is to initiate yourself back into Life, to see what is before you, to live from the unfurnished eye. This means your awareness is no longer cluttered with the stories of struggle that make up the clouds in your head, obscuring the meadow of your being. When your urge to struggle with Life has calmed down and instead you are willing to show up for the life you have been given, you become a force of healing in the world. Wherever you go, you are *here,* and a person who is truly *here* is a focal point of consciousness in this fairly unconscious world.

Humanity urgently needs more and more of us who are willing to open to Life. The collective mind of humanity is deeply caught in the clouds of a conceptual worldview. All of the unskillful actions on our planet and the heartache that ensues come from human beings who are not here for Life. They are so caught in their fear-based clouds of struggle that they act from hatred, domination, greed, victimhood, and violence. They become so lost in their struggles that they can destroy their lives and impact the lives of many other people too.

The suffering that is created by unconscious human beings is enormous. The National Institute on Drug Abuse reports that fifty-two million people in the United States aged twelve and older have used prescription medication for nonmedical reasons. That doesn't even include all of the rampant abuse of nonprescription drugs, alcohol, cigarettes, food, credit cards, the Internet, and other addictive things. The fallout from being lost in our clouds of struggle also includes physical, mental, emotional, and sexual abuse, along with all of the attempts to manage the pain of the abuse, including hoarding, self-cutting, and violence.

Let's not forget the many wars happening right now on our planet and all of the consequences that children, women, and men are suffering. Then there is Earth itself with its soil, water, and atmosphere polluted from our inability to see the sacredness of every single thing.

Let's include your life too. You, like most people, are probably living in a chronic, low-grade stream of struggle that sometimes flares up into bigger struggles. Instead of feeling the joy of being alive, you feel the weight of it. You may even be experiencing some of the suffering described in the last two paragraphs.

No matter how much you are struggling with what is showing up in your life, there is a way out of the endless game of struggle—not only for you, but for all beings as well. In fact, this time of crisis on our planet is a breakthrough rather than a breakdown. It holds the possibility that you and many other human beings can finally recognize that who you really are is not the clouds of struggle. You are the awareness that can see and be with your struggles.

A story from Elisabet Sahtouris, an evolutionary biologist, metaphorically illustrates this transformation of our consciousness. She says that, relative to its size, the caterpillar is one of the most destructive beings on this planet. It can devour a whole tree branch in record time. Eventually it weaves a cocoon around itself and, within that structure, fulfills its destiny to dissolve into formless goo. Out of that goo begins to emerge the first cells of the butterfly. These new cells are called imaginal cells, and the goo (the old) tries to destroy them. Because of this threat, the new cells gather together into groups, and in that support, the butterfly is born.

The caterpillar and its self-absorbed destruction represent the old kind of mind that humanity has been living in. The caterpillar is necessary in the creation of the butterfly, but there comes a time when it has to die for the butterfly to be born. The butterfly, which represents the new use of the mind we've been exploring, is the opposite of the caterpillar. It doesn't destroy Life. Instead, it serves Life by pollinating flowers. It can also fly far and wide, so its view is much broader than that of the caterpillar. As we grow into our "butterflyness," we too can have a view that includes everything.

So know that, no matter what is happening in your life, you are an imaginal cell. You are a part of the shift from separation to connection that is happening on our planet, and your life matters. It makes a difference how you choose to be with your life. I love to say that the oceans are made out of drops of water. Which drop isn't important? You are a drop of water in the ocean of awakening consciousness that is now happening.

And your actions count. Or as Desmond Tutu, the South African activist who won the Nobel Peace Prize, once said, "Do your little bit of good where you are. It is those little bits of good put together that overwhelm the world." Yes, do good actions, but the most important action you can take is to heal the war inside of you. Have the courage to show up for what Life is showing you and follow the path home to your heart.

As you clear the pathway from unconsciousness to consciousness for yourself, you also are clearing it for the world. Every moment you relate to what Life is offering you rather than from it, every moment that you are curious about what is unfolding rather than trying to control it, every moment you meet yourself and all beings with the spaciousness of your aware heart, every moment you recognize that what's in the way *is* the way, and every moment you reconnect with the pure joy of being alive, you become a healing presence in the world. I found a quote, attributed to Albert Einstein, that said, "There are only two ways to live your life: one is as though nothing is a miracle; the other is as though everything is a miracle."

> ❦ Use your imagination to open up to this new era of possibility on our planet. In your imagination, see our beautiful planet completely dark. Now see that a few thousand years ago, a light turns on somewhere on the planet: the light of an awake heart. As the years unfold, see more and more lights turning on as more and more hearts wake up. See these individual lights beginning to create a web of light all over the planet that shines into the pockets of darkness that still exist. Then see this all unfolding into a place where our planet fully shines, without one molecule of existence excluded from the healing of the heart. ❧

This healing is possible, and you are an essential part of this healing. How you live your life matters!

I would like to end by coming back to what I said at the end of the introduction: On behalf of all the people who live on this beautiful, blue-green jewel that is our planet, I thank you for your willingness to take this journey back to Life. This gratitude comes from knowing that as you discover and live from the meadow of well-being, your life will be transformed. And as your life transforms, you will transform the lives of everyone you meet—or even think about—for the rest of your life. When you are not caught in the world of struggle, you are here, open to the amazing majesty and mystery of Life, radiating the presence of well-being. And a human being who has discovered how to be here becomes an invitation to all beings to unhook from the mind's addiction to struggle and to open into the joy of being fully here for Life.

For your healing and the healing of all beings, Life is bringing you home.

Appendix
The Eight Spells and Their Variations

Below is the list of the eight core spells introduced in chapter 4 and the different ways your storyteller can say them in your head. Check off the variations that you are familiar with and you will have a greater sense of the world of your storyteller. At the end of the list, the spells are in a circle so you can see that they are a circular continuum.

THE TWO FOUNDATIONAL SPELLS

1. I am separate from Life.
____ Life is only what you see.
____ There is me in here and life out there.
____ I am my thoughts.
____ I am this mind-made me.

2. Life is not safe.
____ Life rejects me.
____ Life abandons me.
____ It overtakes me.
____ There won't be enough.
____ There will be too much.
____ It is hard.
____ I can't trust Life.
____ I must run away/hide.
____ Life happens to me.

___ Life is overwhelming.

___ There is no protection.

___ Life is dangerous.

___ Something bad will happen.

___ Life is not fair.

___ Life will not support me.

___ I can't count on anything.

THE THREE OPERATIONAL SPELLS

3. I must control Life.

___ I must *do* Life.

___ I must resist what I don't like.

___ I must hold on to what I do like.

___ I create my reality.

___ I've got it together.

___ I am in charge.

___ I won't. . . .

___ I am the best.

___ I will do it later.

___ Get over it.

___ It's no big thing.

___ I can control how others feel about me.

___ I need to understand.

___ I will hurt you.

___ I need to be prepared.

___ I will not look at what I am experiencing.

___ I must get to my goal.

___ I must control you.

___ You are the cause of my problems.

___ My life needs to be different.

___ I need to be different.

___ It is my responsibility.

___ You need to be what I need you to be.

___ I will be happy when. . . .

___ The love I want comes from outside of me.
___ You will not control me.
___ It is your fault.
___ I'm the only one who can take care of me.
___ I don't want to be seen.

4. I must do it right.
___ I must be perfect.
___ I must be cool/together.
___ I must be on top of it.
___ I can't be authentic.
___ I am doing it right.
___ It is not okay to make a mistake.
___ I have to be right.
___ I will be what others need me to be.
___ I am better than you.
___ I must please you.
___ I won't be wrong.
___ I have to be best.
___ I must find the right answer.
___ My life will be over if I don't. . . .
___ I can't look stupid.
___ If I . . . I'll get into trouble.
___ I have to do it all myself.

5. I am not doing it right enough.
___ I am too much.
___ I am less than.
___ I am going to do it wrong.
___ Everybody else does it right.
___ It's my fault.
___ I sabotage myself.
___ I am lazy.
___ I am a procrastinator.
___ I don't know how.

___ I am not trying hard enough.

___ I should have done it differently.

___ I am on the wrong path.

___ I am wasting time.

___ It is not working.

___ I look foolish.

___ I am scared.

___ This is taking too long.

___ I didn't live up to their expectations.

___ I am boring.

___ I should have done it earlier.

___ I don't look good/right.

___ I can't concentrate/focus.

___ I make too many mistakes.

___ I didn't get what everybody else got.

___ I don't know how to do my life.

___ I don't perform the way they want me to.

___ I should be happy/grateful.

___ This will keep on happening.

THE THREE HIDDEN SPELLS

6. I am wrong.

___ I am worthless.

___ I am bad/evil.

___ I am stupid.

___ I am a failure.

___ I don't belong.

___ I won't be able to ever get it together.

___ I am wrong to my core.

___ I am a fake.

___ I am a loser.

___ I can't change.

___ I can't change things.

___ I hate myself.

___ I didn't live up to my potential.

___ I hate what I am doing.

___ I have no value.

___ I am a mistake.

___ I am helpless.

___ I am inadequate.

___ I've got to do it better.

___ It's not okay to feel what I feel.

___ Life is out to get me.

___ I will be found out.

___ I don't deserve to be happy.

___ I have run out of time.

___ I missed my chance.

___ I get what I deserve.

___ I can't figure anything out.

___ I don't fit in.

___ I am not what others want me to be.

___ Everyone else has it together.

7. I am unlovable.

___ I don't matter.

___ I don't deserve this.

___ I am not worthy.

___ I will be rejected.

___ Nobody will take care of me.

___ Nobody likes me.

___ I am not good enough.

___ Nobody chose me.

___ I don't deserve to exist.

___ I have no value.

___ I'll never feel loved.

___ They don't really love me.

8. I am all alone.

___ This is all there is.

___ Despair is all there is.

___ This will last forever.

___ I am depressed.

___ I am lonely.

___ I don't know who I am.

___ Things will never change.

___ I feel left out.

___ I don't exist.

___ I don't want to live.

___ I will never get what I need.

___ There is no way out.

___ I am invisible.

___ Nothing is real.

___ I can't do this anymore.

___ I don't want to do this anymore.

___ I am trapped.

___ I want to die.

___ There is no space for me.

___ I don't fit in.

___ No one else cares if I live or die.

___ No one is here for me.

___ Everybody rejects me.

___ There is no hope for me.

___ I need to leave to make it safe.

The Circle of Spells

Acknowledgments

It takes a village to birth a book! Besides MarySue Brooks, who is my business partner and heart sister on this amazing journey called Life, there have been countless others who have supported this work. I host four ongoing groups that have been the incubators of the essence of what is being offered here, and I thank each and every person who has been, is right now, or will be a part of one of the groups. This is also true of everybody I have worked with on an individual basis in the past thirty years, for healing happens when two people show up together in curiosity and compassion. And I am deeply grateful for the people who were willing to share their stories for this book. They enhanced it deeply.

I also thank my children, Katrina and Micah, for doing such a good job in raising me. I grew with, for, and because of them!

Words cannot describe my gratitude for my publicist and friend Martha Logan's endless hours and amazing creativity in finding avenues for spreading the message in this book. Her life was transformed by this work and, as a result, she has a passion to share the work with the world.

My dear friend Stephanie Kerns is an essential part of this unfolding. Not only has she been my retreat manager, but it is also with her that I learned the art of true friendship.

I feel deep gratitude for Mark Ricker, who keeps our computers in top form, and the two in-person groups who lived the Remembering Sessions and helped to fine-tune them.

About the Author

Mary O'Malley is a speaker, author, group facilitator, and counselor in private practice in Kirkland, Washington. For more than thirty years, she has explored and practiced the art of being truly present for Life. Through her organization, Awakening, she invites others into a center of clarity, compassion, and trust that can be accessed no matter what is happening in their lives. She offers an invitation to live from the place in which the impossible becomes possible and our hearts soar with the joy of being alive.

Mary offers audio CDs, three other books, engagements, retreats, workshops, phone and in-person counseling, and phone and in-person groups. For more information, please visit maryomalley.com.

About Sounds True

Sounds True is a multimedia publisher whose mission is to inspire and support personal transformation and spiritual awakening. Founded in 1985 and located in Boulder, Colorado, we work with many of the leading spiritual teachers, thinkers, healers, and visionary artists of our time. We strive with every title to preserve the essential "living wisdom" of the author or artist. It is our goal to create products that not only provide information to a reader or listener, but that also embody the quality of a wisdom transmission.

For those seeking genuine transformation, Sounds True is your trusted partner. At SoundsTrue.com you will find a wealth of free resources to support your journey, including exclusive weekly audio interviews, free downloads, interactive learning tools, and other special savings on all our titles.

To learn more, please visit SoundsTrue.com/freegifts or call us toll free at 800-333-9185.